NICK KOMODINA

SURRENDER

SURRENDER

SURRENDER

SURRENDER

SURRENDER

Letting Go to Level Up

amplify
an imprint of Amplify Publishing Group

amplify
an imprint of Amplify Publishing Group

www.amplifypublishinggroup.com

Surrender: Letting Go to Level Up

The author has tried to recreate events, locales, and conversations from his memories of them. In order to maintain their anonymity in some instances he has changed the names of individuals and places. He may have changed some identifying characteristics and details such as physical properties, occupations, and places of residence.

While the author and publisher have taken great care to ensure the accuracy of the information in this book, they do not assume responsibility for any errors, omissions, or consequences arising from the use of this material, whether due to negligence, accident, or any other cause. This book is not a substitute for medical advice from a qualified healthcare professional. Readers are advised to consult their physicians regarding any health concerns or symptoms requiring diagnosis or medical attention. The views and opinions expressed herein belong solely to the author and do not necessarily reflect those of the publisher or its staff.

This book includes detailed depictions of attempted suicide. If you or someone you know is struggling, please seek help. In the US, you can contact the Suicide & Crisis Lifeline by dialing 988.

For more information, please contact:
Amplify Publishing, an imprint of Amplify Publishing Group
620 Herndon Parkway, Suite 220
Herndon, VA 20170
info@amplifypublishing.com

Library of Congress Control Number: 2025909897

CPSIA Code: PRV0725A

ISBN-13: 979-8-89138-104-9

Printed in the United States

CONTENTS

PROLOGUE

I rolled over in bed to look at my phone on the nightstand: 34 percent battery, 2:47 a.m. My eyes burned from exhaustion; my chest was clenched with anxiety. The pain through my whole body was indescribable. Just pure suffering.

I sat up and looked around the room. My girlfriend, who had become my ex a few hours earlier, was lying there asleep.

Is this really it? I thought to myself.

How could I have let all this happen? Why didn't I see this coming? Why did this have to happen to me? What is going to happen? I have nothing.

I didn't want to feel that weight anymore. I leaned over the side of the bed and pulled the storage drawer open. There was my gun case, staring back at me. The left lock was cracked, so it was never fully closed.

I put my knees on the floor and carefully opened the case. I could barely see the gun through the tears in my eyes.

Maybe I can be a martyr, I convinced myself. *Yes. That way people can learn from this and avoid all the same mistakes I have made. That would at least let me keep some honor and leave this world with a small fraction of something worthwhile.*

I opened my phone and wrote my suicide letter in the notes.

"That should cover everyone," I whispered to myself.

I locked my phone, put it quietly back on the nightstand, and walked into the backyard with my gun.

It was cold. I was in my underwear. I remember the wind hitting my chest and thinking I should probably go grab a hoodie . . .

"What's the point of that?" I said.

I stared up into the sky as if I was waiting for someone to tell me to stop or tell me it was going to be okay, but nobody was there. It was just me. I looked down at the gun in my hand and watched as my thumb pulled back the trigger, hearing the click as it locked into place. My heart was pounding. I took a deep, crackly breath in as I lifted the gun and pressed it against my temple.

"Holy shit. Fuck. Fuck . . . fuck . . . fuck," I whispered. My knees were shaking. My whole body trembled.

I felt my finger tighten around the trigger as if I was stuck in slow motion. I felt that I was squeezing that trigger for hours.

Then I heard something . . . or maybe someone.

INTRODUCTION

The hardest part of any new endeavor is knowing where to start.

I was born in Escondido, which is a smaller sub-city around San Diego, California. Soon after my birth, the doctors discovered that I had a birth defect consisting of duplicated ureter tubes. (Yeah, I'm not too sure either.) Consequently, I had to undergo my first major surgery at the age of two. I can still vividly see the doctors shoving a needle somewhere that needles should not be shoved and can still smell the cold metal in the room.

This surgery ended with collateral damage to both of my kidneys, rendering them at a function of 50 percent capacity each. Meaning if one fails, the other fails with it. I die. Great.

My mother and I lived in Escondido for a few years. One of our neighbors was a police officer with a K-9 unit. One day we were all outside and the dog barked, startling my young self. When I started to run, the dog chased after me. It attacked me and bit my head completely open. My mother had to literally hold my head together with her hands until the ambulance came to take me to the hospital. Gross, I know.

I actually still remember it. Well, part of it. I remember my body going completely numb; I felt zero pain the entire time. My eyesight went red and then pitch black, kind of like those old

007 games when the character dies. When I woke up, I had fifty staples down the center of my head holding it together. Awesome.

So, by the age of four, I was a regular at the hospital, I had gone through a major surgery, and I had experienced a major head trauma. This whole being-a-human thing didn't seem like it was working out for me.

My mother sacrificed everything for me, so my life had everything it needed, and she did an amazing job. We lived in a trailer park in the outskirts of California, in a town called Santa Ysabel, across the street from good old Lake Henshaw. This is where I lived out my childhood.

Our trailer had a small addition built onto it, maybe two hundred square feet at most. The bathroom was so small I could run the sink, open the door, and touch the furthest wall of the shower all from sitting on the toilet seat. It wasn't much, but it was home.

Home isn't a place; home is a feeling, a safety, a security. You can feel at home with a person. We have all felt this. I felt at home every single day I lived in that trailer park because my mother made it feel like one. If you haven't done it today, put down this book and call your mother to tell her you love her. Moms are nothing short of superheroes, and they deserve the recognition.

From an early age, I was constantly searching for things to learn. I found my first real passion in the form of dinosaurs. Yes, I was the kid who made the roaring noises at recess.

School and learning were not hard for me to pick up. In kindergarten I was already reading at a twelfth-grade level. I loved books. The Harry Potter and Lord of the Rings books were my absolute favorites, outside of dinosaur books, of course.

Soon, I became disinterested in the curriculum at school. I just didn't really care about it. It didn't spark any passion or fire in me; all I wanted to do was read about dinosaurs.

So, I thought to myself, *if I get really good at schoolwork and get it done super fast, then I'll have more time to read about dinosaurs.*

My passion had become motivation for me to get through my workload of school assignments. So that's what I did. I got really good at school. I taught myself how to do math problems in my head so I could save time by not writing out all the work on paper. I earned 100 percent and A's on all my work, every single time.

Unsurprisingly, my teachers started having an issue with me not showing my work. That's the way it's supposed to be done. Get your problems, write out your work on the side, and then find your answer. When I told them I would just do the math in my head, they accused me of cheating. They phoned home, my mom got involved . . . it was a whole ordeal. They made me take a math test in the principal's office to "prove" I was cheating. When I completed the test without missing any questions, I was told that I still needed to do it their way or I would fail.

You are going to encounter strong opinions and hard truths in this book. Here's the first: Our schooling system is tailored around conformity, and we have no curriculum that empowers the creative mind. We get taught one way as if that's the only way there is. It is a system created to reward convergent thinking and to dismiss divergent thinkers.

Teachers are underpaid, and the majority are unmotivated due to that lack of compensation. A rigid system is easier than a student-centered touch.

When a creative child is uninspired, the brain wanders. Instead of the school system stepping up to the plate to accommodate such incredible gifts, we label kids with ADHD and medicate them to conform. I realize this is a bit of a heated stance, but this is my own personal opinion. I'm not here to offend anybody, but I'm not here to water down my takes either. The fact is, I think ADHD is a superpower; you just have to give someone the tools to harness it. Show me a boy who can't pay attention because he has ADHD. Now let's put him in front of a video game he loves and watch him not blink for an hour. This is because when someone who "has ADHD" is not using their power to its full potential—because it is not being directed into a passion—that power goes ballistic. These gifted humans are in need of high intellectual stimulation because they are so powerful. If you can learn to focus it, you can turn it into the superpower that I believe it to be. To my "ADHD people" reading this book: You are powerful. There is nothing wrong with you. You have a gift.

For my part, I lost interest in school altogether. I was no longer allowed to read my dinosaur books because I started failing my tests and homework.

They say that "idle hands are the devil's playground," and they are absolutely right. I no longer had a creative space for an outlet, so I started getting into trouble. Math became my worst subject by far because my brain didn't fit the lock they were trying to force it through. I turned into the class clown, started getting in fights on the playground, turned into a regular in the principal's office, and had a target painted on my back for the rest of my school career.

The schooling system had successfully broken me and turned me into nothing short of a degenerate by the age of eight. I never grew up with a father in my home, so they used that as the explanation for why I acted the way that I did.

I lost interest in dinosaurs, in reading, in anything that had creativity attached to it. My fire had been put out, and to the natural-born creative, that is a fate worse than death. I always wonder how many more Elon Musks there could be today if the school system was more attuned to harnessing a student's natural gifts.

My mother always made me work for money, no matter what. For that lesson, I will be eternally grateful. It has allowed me to create the life I currently have. But when I was growing up, cutting corners was my full-time job. I always tried to find a way to do the least amount possible but still get rewarded.

My mother would have me pull weeds in the front, back, and side yards. Once I finished, she would hand me three quarters so I could run down to the store to buy a bag of Skittles. I distinctly remember a particular day of pulling weeds. The store was about fifteen minutes from closing. I was frantically trying to get all these weeds pulled so I could get my fix (my mom was inadvertently raising a sugar addict).

So, I did what I thought was tactical: I took all the weeds I had pulled and piled them up on top of the weeds I still needed to pull. The job looked done, and I had saved about ten minutes of work. I went and asked my employer for my compensation. With a frantic sense of urgency in my mind, I felt the three coins touch my hand. I sprinted down the hill of our trailer park over to the store. One minute before closing, I burst through the door and made straight for the second aisle and the Skittles boxes. When I went to the cash register, the clerk rang up the Skittles.

"Seventy-five cents, please."

I put my hand out to pay and opened my grip on the coins. I was met with pure shock and outrage. Two quarters and a nickel were sitting in my palm. I didn't have enough.

The clerk asked me to put the Skittles back and to head out since they were about to close. I obliged. With rage running all the way down through my feet, I stomped my way back up to my trailer, where my mom was sitting in her green patio chair out in the sun.

I conveyed my anger about how I wasn't able to buy my Skittles. She said nothing but calmly shifted her gaze over to the far side of the yard. She had cleaned up all my pulled weeds, revealing the ones that had been left in the ground.

"You can't expect to be fully compensated for work you did not fully do," she said, and went back inside.

Needless to say, I picked the rest of the weeds, and my mom handed me two dimes when I came back in.

The lesson I learned that day has been burned into my subconscious ever since. How you do things determines how you get compensated. I gave a half-ass effort; I got half-ass results in return. Life is the compounding effect of our actions, words, and thoughts that manifests itself before our eyes every single day. Until you choose to put integrity behind your "how," you will always be left unsatisfied with your lack of fulfillment and compensation. You cannot expect to be fully compensated for work you did not fully do. Thanks, Mom.

That was by no means (by NO means!) the last hard lesson I learned in my life, but it sets us up to talk about what we're really here to talk about: you.

If you are reading this, you are probably one of two kinds of people. 1) You have your shit together and are doing exactly what you were put on this earth to do. You want to read this book to further that journey. Or 2) you constantly feel that you have a higher purpose, but you just don't know what that is yet, and you're hoping you can find the answer here.

For both types, here's the key that will unlock the potential of this book (and you have my mom to thank for it): our purpose is not tied to what we do—it is tied to how we do what we do. That's it. Your purpose is to give your full potential to whatever is in front of you in your life right now. When we embrace that, what we do starts to become irrelevant, because we start to see that success is an accumulation of common things done in an uncommon way.

When we start to operate this way, laziness and short selling vanish. Simply put, you stop sucking at things. Sucking is the new normal in today's society; not coincidentally, so is complaining about not being where you want to be. If you continue to suck where you are, you will stay stuck where you are. Period. Let's break out of that cycle together. Here's how.

THE STRAIGHT A'S OF SURRENDER

What is your mission? Who are you meant to help? For what purpose?

As a business/life/spirituality/whatever else coach (I hate these terms, so I use them loosely), one of the first things I help the entrepreneurs I work with figure out before they start their business is finding the people they are meant to serve. Finding the person you were meant to help, figuring out how you can help them, and discerning why they should trust you. This is one of the first things we focus on, but it is far from the first.

Throughout my time working with individuals ranging from first-time business owners to employees at dead-end jobs desperate for a new life all the way to professional athletes and CEOs running billion-dollar companies, I recorded a lot of data. What I started to notice was that there was a series of stages every individual takes to reach the next level of success in their lives. The more I tried to prove my method wrong, the more I believed in it. This method has now become the backbone of my entire life's work.

After my rotten trip to the principal's office, I was never a straight-A student again. My goal now is to become a straight-A student in life. But this grading metric doesn't come down to an individual's perfection, score, or ability to stay within the lines. This is about an individual's willingness to surrender to whatever phase they find themselves in while understanding that the phases are cyclical and continuously repeat.

This method has helped me and countless others step into the truest version of ourselves, and I hope that it can do the same for you. These seven stages are the Straight A's of Surrender.

Asleep
Awareness
Acceptance
Awakening
Application
Ascension
Abundance

I've found that every person at any given time is experiencing one of these stages. Learning to tap into where you are and what you need to do to move forward is the fun part.

This method has helped me and many others unlock higher experiences, greater understandings of self, and increased levels of fulfillment, joy, and gratitude in our lives. It has also generated more wealth across the board than I even know how to categorize.

It is my hope that the Straight A's of Surrender can serve you just as well as they have served me.

A CONFESSION

I didn't love myself when I started writing this book. In fact, it was quite the opposite. I hoped this book would save the public perception of me from my past mistakes and offer me salvation. The original intention was not pure; it was rushed, manipulative, and judgmental—all qualities absent of love. As I've continued to make my way through writing, I have also made my way closer to love. I've had to smooth out the sharp edges of myself that I was convinced I needed in order to survive. I've had to let go of every false identity I lived by throughout my life. It amounted to constantly experiencing what felt like death, over and over again.

Each time bringing me closer to my knees.

I fought through every death cycle to try and hold onto the things I didn't want to let go of, trying to stand up to the universe and prove to God that He had it wrong this time. If you resist when God is asking you to get on your knees so He can save you, you will always feel like the weight of the world is on your shoulders. Because it is.

The ego convinces you that you have to do it alone, you need to be strong, you need to stick to your guns, you have to keep your guard up to stay protected, you have to cling to people, places, and things. If anyone moves on from you, they're awful and think they're too good for you; when clients leave, it's because they took advantage of you; when a partner ends a relationship, it's because they were narcissistic or toxic. We create a life of delusion because we are unwilling to let go and surrender to love.

I wanted everything to go my way, and very few things did. I had to become a student of surrender. When you finally surrender your life to the powers of the universe around us, you soften and allow yourself to float, just as you would float down a river. Knowing that if your head ever drops below water, God's hand will pull you back up and call you worthy, every time.

Source energy, God's energy, is the energy that lives inside all of us. It's who we actually are . . . the energy and power that can create entire worlds, entire realities. All we have to do is let go of the stories that keep us small.

Let's get started.

CHAPTER 1

ASLEEP

Brian Mark (@therealbrianmark) is an incredible business coach who works specifically within the online fitness industry. In discussing what were then the six Straight A's on his podcast, Brian brought to my attention that there is also a denial phase before people can even begin to have awareness of or acceptance for their situation.

I really appreciated that perspective, and it expanded my own take on how to further empathize with people on any part of their journey. Having added Asleep to the roster, I am fully confident that every single person on the planet is in one of these stages at all times.

What does it mean to be asleep? I think this phase is where we see the majority of people in the world today. Let's dive into the autonomy aspect of human design for a fuller approach.

Your subconscious mind is either your worst enemy or your most valuable asset. The difference between the two lies in your ability to wield it, just as a sword can either be a weapon of death or a symbol of protection. The difference lies in the desire of the swordsman's king—you.

Our minds are genetically engineered to reduce bandwidth with mundane tasks to save as much energy as possible. After a while, you stop having to pay hardly any attention when driving to work. You probably (illegally) spend most of your driving time on your phone and yet somehow (hopefully) make it to the gym. You walk into your home and kick your shoes off the exact same way and put the same meal in the microwave that you always do.

If you were to close your eyes and let your subconscious lead the way, you would perform the same tasks, think the same thoughts, and be at the same spots at the same times every day. We love our routines so much that we allow ourselves to become enslaved to them. So much so that the love for life dies out and turns into dull monotony that has sucked all the life force out of our experience. We stop innovating, we stop being creative, we even stop looking for new things to try because we are slaves to habit.

The world around us is not helping. With phones, apps, delivery services, and automated cars, we are becoming less alive and more robotic every day. With the emergence of AI, I believe robots will be able to "human" better than humans very soon. Or maybe we will be able to "robot" better than robots. I wonder which will come first. Now is not the time to sleep. Now is the time to wake up and become a warrior in the war on unconsciousness. So, how do we start to wake up?

ME, ASLEEP

I was in love from the moment I set eyes on her. It was as though there was a voice in my head telling me, *Yes, you know that's her.*

I was at a point in my life where my confidence and swagger were at an all-time high. Yet, when I approached her and she turned around, I froze. Instead of calm and collected words, I made a horrible joke out of context and turned to walk miserably away.

"What the hell did you just do?" I asked myself in utter disbelief. "You blew it."

To my pleasant surprise at the time, she enjoyed my miserable jokes a lot more than they deserved to be enjoyed. We kindled a flame and nurtured that flame into a very powerful fire of love.

We were long-distance, me in San Diego and her in Miami. The complete opposite ends of the continent. We had both recently come out of relationships in which we had experienced infidelity from our partners.

I had made my list of nonnegotiables for a partner and told myself I would never be with someone if these were not all met. Until I met her.

Something happens to our nonnegotiables when we are presented with someone we perceive as "perfect." In short, they start becoming negotiable. But when we set out with our nonnegotiables and start to abandon them, we also abandon ourselves. We are showing ourselves that our integrity falters. We choose to stay asleep.

When we first started dating, she told me she was scared. Scared to be in a full relationship again because of how badly she was hurt. To all of my men reading this, you know the challenge that was accepted in my heart. I would show her that love no longer had to be feared, that love no longer had to hurt. It doomed us from the very start.

One of my nonnegotiables is communication. If you go out, have fun; just let me know once you get home so I know you are safe. This turned into a long-distance argument almost every weekend. I lay in my bed tossing and turning, checking my phone through the burn of my eyes every few minutes—3:05 a.m., 3:10 a.m., 3:27 a.m.—until finally I saw her name pop up on my phone and the anxiety flushed out of my veins for a split second. I became addicted to a high induced by a toxic cycle without even realizing it.

It was routine. It was my life. I was asleep.

In neuro-linguistic programming (NLP), we refer to this as secondary gain, meaning the subconscious gain we get from the problem we consciously have causes us to stay in the toxic cycle and not "want" to break out of it. I continued to spend every weekend tossing and turning, anxiety pulsing through my chest and head until I finally got my dopamine hit of seeing her name pop up on my phone.

So, I allowed my non-negotiable to turn into a negotiable that relied solely on her terms. I had abandoned myself and become a slave to the dopamine hits that validated me—I was still loved and not forgotten.

When we find ourselves in this "settled" position, our power is lost, and it can feel impossible to ever get it back.

As you might imagine, things went from bad to worse. Through a multitude of sketchy interactions and text messages I found between her and other men, I started hyper-analyzing her movements. I started comparing myself to these other men so intensely that I hated myself more and more every day. My self-confidence sank lower and lower as I fought harder to keep up the alpha appearance in front of her and everyone else. I was asleep, but it was not a peaceful sleep.

Desperate for her to just love me and want to be with me, I held on through eight months of constant highs and lows, anxiety, then peace and love, until we finally reached a point where she agreed to be official. Whatever that means nowadays.

I felt an overwhelming sense of accomplishment. *Wow, I have finally done it*, I thought. *I'm "better" than these other men. I won.*

IMPRINTS

I read in an amazing book (*The Diamond Cutter*) about how imprints are generated by every thought, action, and decision we make. These imprints will always lead to an experience, whether good or bad. The way you think, the stories you tell yourself, and even the words you speak out loud to others all create imprints that inevitably generate an experience you must go through. It would've been nice to know that earlier in my life, but hey, pain is the best teacher.

Fast forward a bit, and you will get to the part of the story where this woman and I decided to buy a house together in a state neither of us lived in at the time. We moved for work and for some amazing friends we wanted to be closer to. We bought a big, beautiful house, got a puppy, business was booming, all our friends were there—my life was perfect.

But the imprints created in my subconscious began to grow. I had spent the last year of this relationship constantly filled with anxiety about other men, sketchy texts, unexplained absences, and other very questionable situations . . . and then it all hit me at once.

I am not enough. It's a phrase most of us have told ourselves, one of the most embodied struggles of our entire species—followed by one of the most tragic miscalculations any human being can make: *If I am not enough, then I must self-sabotage.*

So, I did the unthinkable. I cheated. I found myself on a trip, intoxicated, and in a hotel room with another woman. You get the rest.

Love is not a shield from mistakes, demons, or meta-programs in our subconscious. Love is hard. It is not a fairy tale; it is not a newlywed phase until the day you die. Love is a choice, an intention, an act. It takes intention to stay in love with someone forever. But once toxicity bleeds into your love, it will grow if left unattended. It will eventually poison everything in your life, including yourself.

Every time I looked in her eyes, all I saw was myself. I couldn't hold her gaze anymore. Then the internal voice started to speak.

You piece of shit. You are a worthless, cowardly sleaze.

They always tell you to watch what you say because your words have more power than you think. People are the sum total of how you treat them. How you label someone is how they will continue to act. Their reality starts to shift, and their brain starts to create new connections and even develop new habits.

When the person we are speaking harshly to is ourselves, it becomes even more powerful.

So, there I was, filled with shame and guilt while feeding myself nonstop stories about how awful of a human being I was. To negate this, I started entertaining side conversations with no intent behind them other than to get even the slightest dopamine hit to let me know I was still desired or attractive. After each conversation—once the dopamine wore off—more shame and guilt filled its place. I became addicted to the dopamine highs just as much as the shame and guilt lows. I had become addicted to a life that I absolutely hated, and I had no idea.

Asleep, asleep, asleep. How many people suffer from this same subconscious addiction to a life that they hate?

My body became accustomed to functioning on anxious energy. If I didn't feel anxiety, my brain had to find a way to feel it again. It was how I had now been programmed to function. This is something I discovered within myself after this situation finally came to a close.

Once I made my peace, I was exhausted for weeks. I could barely stay awake and function and was sleeping for twelve or more hours at a time. The reason I believe this happens for people is because we release the form of energy our body had become reliant on to function. When you release the anxious, negative energy that has been fueling you for weeks, months, or years, your body does not have any other energy to use for you to function properly. Then there is a "refill phase," as I like to call it. We sleep all day and have a hard time doing anything. Our body is busy refilling our fuel tank with life force energy again.

But that's jumping ahead . . .

A night out with our friends turned into a heart-dropping discovery that she had, in fact, cheated on me as well. With one of my best friends.

To say this rush of emotions was interesting would be a severe understatement. Looking back on it now, I was way harder on her than I should have been. Getting upset with her was easy because I was able to direct some of the anger I had for myself onto her.

Then I did what any other person in my odd and fucked-up situation would do—I stayed.

You deserved that, I told myself.

AWARENESS TASK

If people are the sum total of how we treat them, then we are also the sum total of how we treat ourselves. I had adopted the identity of a shady, unworthy, piece-of-shit scumbag, so I kept myself in the environment best suited to that identity. When you create an identity around who you are, you also create an identity around what you deserve. If you're a victim, you will always find opportunities to reinforce your victimhood.

Most of us don't take the time to sit down and get specific about the stories we are telling ourselves, the identities we have created from those stories, and what we tolerate in our lives because of those identities.

Awareness is the first lock on the door to changing our lives.

To audit the current parameters of my life, I usually follow a blueprint like this:

> **Step 1:** Write down the three main pillars of human experience: health, wealth, relationships.
>
> **Step 2:** Under each of these pillars, I write down everything I am tolerating, everything I am only willing to tolerate occasionally, and everything that I find insufferable.

For example, if you know you are forty pounds overweight and you continue to do nothing about it, that is something you are tolerating. Nobody wants to carry around unnecessary body fat; it's not in our DNA. Most people think that they're unhappy because they're overweight, when in reality, they're overweight because they're unhappy. That may be triggering to some, but being aware that it's triggering and leaning into that sensation will show you the truth that you have been avoiding. That is awareness: taking full ownership for everything in your life, good or bad.

You have probably never taken the time to write out, "I am the only one allowing myself to stay overweight. I am tolerating my unhappiness because I am choosing not to change my habits." Maybe while writing this out, you realize that you're still overweight because eating numbed your anxiety during your childhood. Now, every time you feel stressed, instead of sitting in the emotion, you somehow find yourself right back in the kitchen or ordering food from an app. The mere act of writing down what you're tolerating and then assessing the pattern associated with it automatically dissociates you from that pattern. You are no longer "in" the pattern—you are *observing* the pattern. From this space, you can remove the guilt, shame, and frustration you keep forcing on yourself by "not knowing why I can't stop" doing X, Y, or Z.

Maybe you are struggling financially, but you have never actually written out, "I panic every time I think about money, so I never audit my budget or feel empowered to make more. I tolerate my scarcity and accept the story that I will never make enough to be comfortable."

Maybe every relationship you enter ends exactly the same way, and you continue to tolerate red flags because it feels better to have someone to talk to than it feels to be alone.

Write it all down. Take your time—these lists may end up being longer than you think (or would like to admit). For that reason, I recommend using a different sheet of paper for each pillar. Write out as much as you can under each pillar before moving on to Step 3.

> **Step 3:** Write out the stories inside your head when you observe each of these pillars. ("I'm never going to be loved," "I am always the one that bad things happen to," "I am not a good person," "I am a liar, and I don't deserve peace or happiness," . . .)

> **Step 4:** Now write out why you continue to treat yourself this way.

Step 5: Once I have all of these written down, I find my "umbrella identity," the one identity that governs all my patterns, stories, and emotions. Once I realize my umbrella identity says that I am not enough, I know why I am a people pleaser (core), or I never get things done on time (core), or I always get cheated on by my partners (core). Each of these core identities is governed by the umbrella identity, and each comes with its own set of patterns.

Step 6: Choose a new identity. This identity can be anything you desire yourself to be. We waste the majority of our energy focusing on changing a pattern before first establishing a new governing umbrella identity. Rarely do we give ourselves permission to entertain the thought of a desired reality without first watering it down to fit into a construct we believe is "realistic." That's what makes Step 6 so tough.

If I am overweight and lingering in the identity of someone who "never sticks to anything," when I say, "I'm going to start working out and getting in shape," I am creating a pattern that is still governed by the undesired umbrella identity. Which means I will inevitably find myself right back in the same patterns that reinforce the belief that I am not enough.

If your truth is that you "never stick to anything," then trying to stick to something from that truth only ensures you never get past the "trying" portion of it.

In order for a concept to have my full commitment, it has to ring true when I read it both forwards and backwards. "I never stick to anything" becomes

"I always do what I say I'm going to do."

The new pattern now has a governor, something to create an intention. We need not concern ourselves with changing all of these undesired patterns. We need only to choose a new umbrella identity and focus all of our attention (energy) on staying aligned with it.

> **Step 7:** Now that we have all this in our awareness, the final step is to simply put it into action and observe any relapses into your old identity as an objective observer.

I had a scarce identity around money for a large portion of my life. Sometimes that undesired identity finds its way back up and tries to rob me of the present moment. In these moments I simply pause, take a deep conscious breath into my stomach, and ask myself, "Is this how the desired version of you would be reacting? What would the desired version of you do in this situation?"

From there, I simply realign my thoughts and actions with the desired umbrella identity and go about my day.

The more power we give to the things we don't want, the more of them we invite.

Become aware, write, choose what you do want, and let everything else fade away.

"WHY ARE YOU STILL IN THIS RELATIONSHIP?"

My friends asked me this more often than I could ignore. I never had an answer because at that point I truly did not know. This compounded into the heaviest weight of inadequacy, low self-confidence, anxiety, and endless intrusive thoughts. I was unconscious. Fast asleep. I didn't even *know* I was miserable.

Then the voice would come back. That little whisper in the back of my mind that told me . . . *She's going to do it to you again. Why don't you do it too?*

I kept trying to control the situation with constant talks that always led to fights, but it never seemed to improve. I see now that I was shifting into a dictator instead of a leader. I was so set on staying in this relationship that I would not lead myself out of it, even though it was abundantly clear something was going on. It was my routine, my pattern, my identity. Above all else, humans will do almost anything to maintain the identity they have for themselves. We choose to stay stuck because we don't know who we are without the identity associated with our own misery.

I stayed in a situation that no longer served me, trying to change those around me instead of changing myself. I am sure a lot of you reading this can resonate with this. This is what it means to be asleep. Instead of leading ourselves away from situations and relationships that do not serve us, we try to make the other person change because we are scared. The thought of being alone or "losing" a relationship or a situation or a comfort seems more painful than staying in and being miserable. Sometimes letting go feels worse than holding on.

I stopped feeling passion for anything. I was making more money than I had ever made in my life—bought a fancy matte-black Acura NSX, had the perfect home, business was booming, yet I was miserable. My fire for life was gone. My light began to dim; my skin even had a consistent pale shade. I looked sick because deep down I was. I started acting out of impulse instead of discernment. Reacting instead of responding.

Naturally, I fell right back into my dopamine addiction of getting validation from other women in conversations and flirting.

Then I cheated again. Rinse and repeat.

My life became a roller coaster of doing copious amounts of drugs at music festivals every other month, then staying sober when our friend group went out so I could keep an eye on her.

Thank God, it all came to a head eventually. One weekend I had to be four hours away for a bodybuilding show, while all of our friend group went out clubbing. Knowing that they would be together without me left me paralyzed and unfocused. That was the first time in my career I can truly say I let down my athletes by not being fully present, and it still haunts me to this day.

I ended up leaving early to drive back that night to meet them all out at a nightclub.

That car ride was one of the longest of my life. I was driving 120 miles per hour for the majority of it just so I could get there to "save" something. When I showed up to the club, I walked in, and she was in the corner embracing another one of my best friends, alone.

This was the first time I had ever truly yelled at her with anger, which she did not deserve. We drove home and slept in different rooms.

A few days later, one of our friends told me there had been an affair going on for quite some time. As I type this, I can still feel the sensation in my body when I first read that text message. My heart dropped into my stomach, my chest started pounding, and my breathing went short and rapid. I could barely function or stay cognizant of anything around me.

I was a mix of upset, sad, hurt—and relieved. I finally had validation from over a year of suspicion and gaslighting. I knew I wasn't crazy deep down, but to finally have it confirmed was an immense relief.

Nonetheless, at this point I would have walked through

hell to make it work. Even if it meant abandoning more of myself as a man. I was desperate for love. I see now that I was holding onto nothing but a dream of what I thought my life *could have* been. We were slow dancing in a burning room, and we both knew it, but we decided to close that chapter and start to heal and move forward. I forgave her because in the back of my mind I was still haunted by what I had done as well. About two weeks went by, and things started to feel a little more "normal" again.

Then everything hit me at once, *again*—all the voices, all the guilt, all the shame. Her mistakes had come out, and I had started to forgive her, but I was still holding onto mine. That was unfair; it was my responsibility to come clean. But I was mortified at the thought of having that conversation. Deep down I think I knew she was looking for a justification to leave.

My anguish was so intense I would have panic attacks and start sweating profusely. There were even points where our dogs started following me around the house whining because they could feel my energy was so off.

Energy doesn't lie. Energy is the truth, and the truth exists whether we choose to believe it or not.

SET FREE

I finally called my friend Grant, who was also a mentor of mine at the time. I told him everything. It was the first time I had ever let all of that come out of me, and it felt like I dropped fifty pounds in a twenty-minute span. This was my first real eye-opening moment about how much our physiology can change by holding onto trauma and negative emotions.

Grant heard me out, then spoke to me.

"The truth will set you free," he said. "Your truth is all you will ever have; you need to use it."

I will never be able to repay Grant or thank him enough for that conversation. It truly was the catalyst that changed my entire life for the better. It is fascinating to think of the immense domino effect that just one conversation can produce. I never take my encounters or conversations with people lightly anymore because I have seen how impactful they can be—for better and for worse.

I came clean about my infidelity, and I was met with a lot of aggression. To my shame, I did not reveal any of my side conversations or other wrongdoings. In my head, "cheating was the worst, so the others don't really matter." It was a coward's way of speaking the truth.

She told me we could never be together again. I begged and pleaded, but she would not hear me. I agreed to go to Tampa for the week to give each other space. Then we would have a real conversation about what we were going to do.

My last night in that house with her, in our bedroom, as I stood in our doorway and watched her sitting on the floor with her head in her lap, crying, will never leave my brain. I had truly lost everything I thought I had.

That night I watched her as she slept, longing for her to wake up and tell me everything was going to be ok. That brings us to the prologue you read at the beginning of this book.

I went back inside, put the gun away, and quietly got back into bed to try and sleep a few hours before the sun came up. The next day I had to leave for the airport. Deep down, I knew it was goodbye. I just did not want to give up hope.

When you are in fight or flight, your mind is frantically trying to find the "threat" to justify the nervous system response. I kept checking Instagram stories to see what was going on. I became obsessed with finding new information that would hurt me more.

If you go looking for something, you are sure to find it. I found plenty.

I came home a week later to an empty house. I went to our bathroom and looked in the mirror at myself, deranged from a week of self-torture on Instagram. I was horrified at what I had done to myself.

"What the fuck are you doing?" I said.

Finally, I had woken up. I knew what I needed to do, even though I didn't want to. I started packing up my things so I would be gone before she got back.

TOXICITY

Toxic is a word our society knows all too well, or at least, we think we know it well. We see it painted on everything and everyone we don't agree with. Toxic masculinity, toxic people, toxic relationships, toxic jobs, toxic environments, etc. That's all it ever really is, though: painted, never understood.

I found myself in what many, including myself, would describe as a toxic relationship. Now, I want to rewrite that sentence and have you focus on the first three words.

I found myself in what many, including myself, would describe as a toxic relationship.

I found myself.

What if we stopped labeling people and situations as toxic? What if we were able to look through the surface-level smokescreen and find the beauty in the mess that inevitably will become our message later in life? Sometimes toxic situations show us who we are not. Can the human mind ever find true oneness in itself without a foil for comparison?

I had been talked out of a lot of things during this time of my life. Some things that I wish I would have pursued. It was time for me to break away from a life that was causing nothing but pain and put my focus back on my dreams. It was time to be deliberate about how I did things.

You cannot change what you have done or what you have been through, but you can make your future look any way you want it to. That is your path: not continuously wishing the road behind you was different but continuously working to create a better road in front of you.

CHAPTER 2

AWARENESS

Think of the Straight A's as a recovery program for underselling yourself and not living up to your potential. We will call it the Apathetics Anonymous Program. My goal is to help everyone disinterested in their lives to reignite their passions, step into their purpose, and learn how to unlock all of the riches this life has to offer. As I'm writing this . . . that idea doesn't sound half bad.

In any good "program" for recovery, we always start with bringing awareness to the problem. This phase comes paired with a lot of self-reflection and consciously limiting distractions. The first time I ever really understood what it meant to become "aware" was reading *A New Earth* by Eckhart Tolle. In this book, Tolle describes the version of you that is experiencing an emotion and then the version of you that can observe yourself experiencing the emotion. If you were only experiencing the emotion, you would not be aware of the fact that you were experiencing it; you would only have the emotion itself in your awareness.

How can we apply that level of awareness to our own lives and start peeling back the layers of our potential? First, we have to figure out where we are giving most of our energy away. Let's talk about these energy leaks.

ENERGY LEAKS

An energy leak occurs when we allow a hard line that was put in place to protect our energy to blur. If we keep allowing enough leaks over time, we eventually reach exhaustion. Our energy becomes scarce. We have a hard time getting out of bed, we crash at midday, and we need five coffees, an energy drink, and an Adderall to keep us functioning. (Just me?)

Potential energy leaks are all around us, especially with social media. One of the first steps I take with my clients (that's you now!) when we begin cleaning up energy leaks is a mass unfollowing spree on all social media platforms. We do one "rinse through" per day for an entire week.

After day one, the most amazing shift starts to take place. On the first day of unfollowing, they're usually unfollowing "hollow" accounts. People they don't really know or interact with but still pay some of their attention (energy) to by being on their timeline. After the initial rinse, I have them sleep on it until the next day. In just one night, they have already patched multiple energy leaks that they weren't even aware of, and you know what happens? They get better and make firmer decisions almost instantly. Day two, they go in again, and now they unfollow more people, the ones they thought they shouldn't unfollow the day prior. On day three they have even more energy leaks patched up, and the cycle continues. They stop frantically stressing over whether someone is going to be upset or not, and decisions become even easier.

It starts to become addictive how good they feel when they start cleaning up their energy with this small and seemingly mundane task. If one little mundane task has the power to make us feel this good, can you imagine how many other mundane tasks drain our energy and make us feel bad? Things we're *unaware* of?

When we have our energy leaking out of so many different holes for so many years, we find ourselves significantly dysregulated. Our nervous system is unable to handle stress. As we begin to take back our energy piece by piece, we start to feel more regulated. We start to feel more like us again. Which is an unusual feeling when you convince yourself that the lower-energy version of you is normal. It isn't, and it's time to take that power back.

I've observed three places where people typically give away the majority of their power, leaving them feeling weak and helpless. I call these the Three P's of Disem(PPP)owerment. (See what I did there?)

In the Three P's of Disempowerment, people are either giving their power away to the Past, other People, or the Pattern (unconscious programming).

THE PAST

We've all done things we aren't proud of. In this stage we are all our own worst enemy, our harshest critic, and the source of our own frustrations. Maybe there is a certain event in your mind right now. Maybe there are multiple. If your past is your biggest energy sucker, then pick the first accident that comes to mind, and let's start there. And I don't use the word *accident* by accident. (No more dad jokes, I promise.)

I had an amazing conversation with a man at a leadership conference I attended a few weeks back. We talked about accidents. Say you're driving down the freeway and someone slams on their brakes in front of you. It's 2023, so you probably didn't even notice because you were scrolling through TikTok because your attention span is that of a goldfish. Anyway, you slam into the other car, your airbag deploys, your seat belt gives you a burn across your neck, and of course you are most traumatized because you can no longer find your phone.

You're banged up, and your car is wrecked. People validate you by expressing their concern, then you go on about your life. You got what you needed out of this accident: the lesson to be more aware and pay better attention. You accept the pain that it caused you, and you give it the time to heal. Now you are a more aware driver. Even though the accident was your fault for not being *aware* of what was going on, you are more than likely not going to drive back to the same accident spot every day and beat yourself up about what happened, how you could have avoided it, and how unworthy you are of driving ever again. Wreck, share, learn, improve, move on.

Now what happens when we find ourselves in an accident that has to do with how we show up as a human being? Are we still as aware of how the accident is giving us something we need to evolve as a conscious being? Or are we driving by the accident site every day just to remind ourselves of our shortcomings, becoming obsessed with more ways to prove to ourselves just how unworthy we are of love, success, happiness, and acceptance?

This used to be me, not only for myself but for everyone around me. I was filled with judgment for others because I was filled with judgment for myself.

Making mistakes comes with the territory of being human. A sixteen-year-old getting into a car accident from looking at her cell phone is just a kid who has yet to experience enough "accidents" to become more aware. We need mistakes to learn and stretch our consciousness. Pain is the greatest teacher of all, but the lessons won't actually set in until we let go of that pain. The hardest part for anyone is the act of letting go.

We are collectively plagued with regret for mistakes we've made in our past. Everyone is having the same conversations with themselves. "I wish I could have another chance." Wishing you could have one more try, feeling defeated because if you had done one thing differently, everything would have been different . . . but you didn't, and they're not.

When you keep all your attention on the past, your energy follows suit. You never stop anticipating your past, which is why you remain anxious for the future. Learning to observe our past selves with understanding and compassion is key to unlocking our true power. We can't expect to be perfect from the start. The mistakes we make are part of the human experience. We were sent here to learn how to manipulate energy and take control of our reality, not to be helpless victims.

Think about the mistakes you made fifteen years ago. The version of you now, in this more evolved state of consciousness, would probably never make those decisions again. Why? Because the awareness that came from the consequences grew your level of consciousness. We cannot evolve without learning, and we cannot learn without mistakes. I have seen so many incredibly gifted people keep themselves in lower levels of life just because they are unaware of the power they are giving away to a story from their past. If you had not done what you did, you would not be able to be the person you are today with the empathy you now possess. Even more importantly, if you had not done everything you have done, you would not be reading this book right now. If this is where all your choices and mistakes have brought you, I would say you're doing pretty okay!

OTHER PEOPLE

If you are anything like me, you have undoubtedly had your share of relationships that just, well . . . sucked. They never really made you feel good. At best, you tolerated them and maybe still do. You will more than likely have specific people come to mind during this next section. I invite you to take that very seriously as we start to lay out steps to build awareness around energy leaks that may currently be present in your life.

Even thinking about someone having a false perception of us or saying something bad can be enough for us to abandon ourselves entirely. The thought of negative energy being directed toward us by others is so terrifying that we inflict it on ourselves instead. So, we don't have hard conversations. We convince ourselves that we just "aren't good with confrontation." Well, how could we be if we are tapped of the energy that makes us powerful?

The concept of stoplight-coded relationships was brought to life after my therapist planted a seed in my head during one of our sessions about an energy leak. For a very long time, most of my clients had an easy time becoming my "good friends." Which made sense to me back then. I was attracting like-minded people. We thought the same and shared interests. Why wouldn't that grow into a friendship over time? You know what I was really doing? Blurring lines that needed to be firm in order to protect my energy. As the line between client and friend started to blur, my authority would start to diminish, eventually leading to the client leaving my services to go elsewhere. Which, because my energy was leaking everywhere, left me taking it as a personal attack and feeling as though I had been betrayed by a friend. Can you say, "abandonment wounds"?

Why would I continue to let that cycle play out over and over again? Answer: Because I didn't have a core group of friends that I had bonded deeply with and consciously poured energy into building a real relationship with. I was always open to more friendships because I never knew how to keep any. I cycled through friends like they were breath mints. (I eat breath mints very fast.) I had no energy to give when it came to building a friendship, let alone a relationship. Deepening a connection with someone, platonic or romantic, takes energy. It takes conscious effort, it takes hard conversations, it takes vulnerability—and sometimes a debilitating amount of humility. I didn't have enough energy to make hard decisions for myself, so I allowed my external environment to make them for me.

I was terrified to set boundaries with my clients because I thought if I wasn't being everything for them, they would leave. I would constantly try to be everything for everyone because I was desperate for someone to be everything for me. I did not know how to be everything for myself. It was an incredibly lonely time in my life. As I began to set boundaries and uphold new standards for where I directed my energy and how much of it I gave, things started shifting fast. I had clients discontinue when they felt I no longer cared about them as much; then it took even more energy to not feel the need to justify myself. That was tough, but I was cleaning my energy, and in doing so, I had to start running firm audits for everyone in my life, myself included.

Remember when I told you at the beginning of this section that people were going to come to your mind? Here we go. Grab a pen and paper (or the notes app on your phone, because most of us have probably forgotten how to write on paper at this point). I want you to write down everyone who comes to mind in the three sections: green light, yellow light, and red light.

GREEN LIGHT RELATIONSHIPS

A green light relationship is a genuine mutual friendship. This level of friendship is just as crucial inside a romantic relationship as well. For the sake of not ping-ponging between the two, we are just going to focus on platonic friendships for these examples.

A green light relationship must be a co-upliftment. I actively choose to do my part in lifting you up, and you actively choose to do your part in lifting me up. In these relationships, we understand the other on a deeper level of their humanity as they continue to help us understand deeper parts of our own. We ease back on trying to be a "good friend" and relax into our real selves. There is no need for masks or performances. You can both be your authentic self in your entirety. These friendships, while the most challenging at times due to the higher level of conscious involvement, have the ability to make us feel fully free. They empower us to be better, to look inward at our shit while being held in an unconditional container of love and acceptance. These relationships are rarely 50/50. Sometimes they are 100/0 when one of you is in a heavy season of their life. Sometimes they are 60/40, 20/80, and everything in between.

Something I love about these relationships is that they also fully embody the energetic signature of abundance. They teach a lesson about what it means to be wealthy. These are the relationships where you aren't keeping tabs on who has done what for whom. You aren't frantically splitting the bills down to the penny every time you go out. An act of kindness equals an act of kindness, and there is nothing more or less in comparison. It is a commitment to enriching the experience for both of you, even when sometimes that means having really hard conversations and dealing with triggers. You are giving freely because the love between you brings out your natural energy of generosity. Trauma will come up to be processed a lot in these relationships because we continue to let ourselves be seen in deeper, more intimate ways. This was the point in friendships where I would usually turn and run because I didn't want them to see what was underneath. If it was as bad as I thought, it was almost a sure thing (in my head) that my friend would see it and abandon me. I couldn't let other people see me because I was unwilling to fully see myself.

When the light is green, that's the sign to keep moving forward. In green light relationships, you both must continue to move forward with the deepening of the connection. This is why green light relationships are harder to maintain; they require a severe level of conscious effort and co-regulation. When you start to prioritize green light relationships in your life, you will realize very quickly that the other relationships do not deserve the same access to your energy anymore.

I used to think I needed to have a large circle of friends in order to be safe. That was only because I had no green light relationships and had to keep shifting through friend groups like a wanderer. I also didn't realize that I hadn't created a green light relationship with myself yet. It was hard for me to keep moving forward in any relationship after a certain point. When you finally get your car onto the freeway, but you stop moving forward, catastrophe is sure to follow. I was a collision-in-waiting in every friendship I found myself in because I had not understood how to keep my foot on the gas while keeping my focus on my desired destination. Which was home.

Green light friendships become our home, which is why it's so crucial to create one with yourself first. If you can't sit at home with yourself, you will never be able to sit at home with someone else. Here are a few questions I ask myself to assess if a relationship is in the green light zone: (Note: if even one of these boxes is a no, then it is not a green light for me.)

- ☐ Does this person make me feel completely seen, heard, and understood?
- ☐ Am I able to confide in them without hesitation or fear of judgment?
- ☐ Do I trust them with every dark part of my truth?
- ☐ Do I feel better energetically when I am with them?
- ☐ Do I make them feel better energetically when I am with them?
- ☐ Do we both enjoy making the extra effort to make the other feel loved? (Words of affirmation, small gifts, invitations to hang out, etc.)
- ☐ Can we have hard conversations if mistakes are made or boundaries accidentally get crossed?
- ☐ Do we avoid or do we engage when things feel off?
- ☐ Do we feel like home to each other?

If these are all marked as yes, then this is a green light relationship and deserves the bulk of your conscious effort into nurturing it further. We want to expend 90 percent of our energy on green light relationships, as they will turn into your core people that provide for you everything you could ever need in a community. When you have your core people with whom you have nurtured deep, intimate relationships, you are able to set hard lines in other areas of your life because you no longer *need* more friends. You are more aware of how special your energy is because it is used to breathe life into the people who breathe life back into you. Green light relationships help us clean up energy leaks and step back into our truest power.

If you have relationships in your life that are in the green light, take a second to send them a message along these lines:

"Hey _____, I'm currently reading this book, *Surrender*, written by the devilishly handsome author Nick Komodina. I think you should buy fifteen of them and hand them out."

Okay, maybe not that, but I would invite you to take out your phone and spend the next ten minutes sending gratitude and acknowledgment texts to your core group of people, making a declaration that you desire to start pouring more energy into the relationship to deepen your bond. When you send this, you need to make sure your words are not hollow. Hollow words are a massive energy leak and cause distrust in relationships. If you are going to make the declaration to start consciously nurturing your friendships, you have to mean it. Otherwise, it will turn into a relationship in the yellow zone very quickly.

YELLOW LIGHT RELATIONSHIPS

A yellow light relationship can be perceived as a relationship that feels one-sided most of the time. I used to have a plethora of yellow light friendships. These friends would hit me up when they needed something and then vanish for weeks or months. If I reached out, they were usually busy. Once they needed me again—poof—there they were!

It was normal for most of my friends to come to me for some sort of advice. I had become the friend that everyone would go to when they needed help, support, or guidance. At the time, this made me feel really good because it meant they saw value in me for what I could provide or for the knowledge that I possessed.

What I didn't realize was that I was starting to plant seeds of resentment in my heart. My advice and support would get shorter as I got more annoyed. I started to feel used and undervalued by the people in my life.

In fact, I started feeling like I didn't have any friends at all. I had morphed myself into a pillar for everyone to lean on, a place for everyone to dump the energy they no longer wanted and fill back up on what little energy I had left to give. The praise for always being a safe space and always being there for them had me hooked. One of my love languages is words of affirmation, and I crave it often to feel loved by my people. I put myself in a position where I was abandoning almost every part of myself just to get words of praise to make me feel loved—because I felt anything but.

The reason I felt this way was because I was neither protecting my energy nor practicing self-love. I was in a yellow light relationship with myself. I would come back and nurture my needs when I finally needed to, but when my body came asking me to put up a boundary, I was too busy seeking external praise. Once I reached my tipping point of stress and overwhelm, back I went to myself to love and re-nurture. The bitterness seeds I had continuously planted for myself were starting to grow into a forest of internal self-hate and neglect. Since I had chosen to invite all of my friendships into the yellow zone, I didn't have anybody I could go to for support or guidance. My only option at the time was to bottle it all up, put on a smile, and continue to be there for everyone. I couldn't let them know I was struggling; I was all they had. Being used can look and feel a lot like being loved when you don't know the difference.

In a yellow light relationship, we can abandon ourselves very quickly by prioritizing the other person's well-being over our own. Which eventually serves neither. We aren't holding either to a higher level of integrity by enabling a relationship to stay in the yellow zone.

A yellow light is the sign to start slowing down. Most of us have an instinctual response when we see a yellow light; we either slow down to meet the red light or we speed up to beat the red light. When we feel a friendship turning yellow, it is time for us to either slow down or mutually agree to put in more effort to get it back into the green zone. This can be a great time to take some space and re-evaluate whether or not you are both able to get your needs met in the friendship. If we continue to put our energy toward relationships in the yellow zone, then we are going to start attracting more of them.

There is a flipside to friendships in this zone—a more positive one. This can be how a lot of great friendships actually start in the beginning. Humans are hilarious because we are naturally awkward and create stories about everything. So, in an early stage of meeting someone and sparking a connection, there may be very limited topics that a person feels comfortable using to reach out to connect. A relationship starting in yellow territory is actually pretty normal. It would be odd to jump into every new connection as an immediate green light. We have to take a little bit of time and ease into it to make sure the connection can serve both parties to the highest degree.

The other may only feel comfortable at first reaching out to connect to ask you a question on something that is of mutual interest. We use ways that feel most comfortable to us to connect with others. This is a big part of what I teach the entrepreneurs I work with when it comes to sharing more of themselves on their social media. People love to connect on mutual ground; it gives us a window of opportunity to express sameness with those we admire. So, in this instance, a yellow zone friendship can be a very innocent way to further a connection that will eventually blossom into a green light friendship.

If you have been in a yellow light friendship for an elongated period of time and a lot of your current relationships reflect yellow light characteristics (Who did you think of when reading this section?), then it might be time to take a step back into your own energy for a few days or weeks so you can reassess if your needs are being met.

Here are some questions I ask myself to evaluate if I am in a yellow light friendship:

- ☐ Am I only hearing from them when they need something?
- ☐ Are they only hearing from me when I need something?
- ☐ Do we both walk away from our interactions with higher energy or just one of us?
- ☐ Are they actively checking in on me to see how I am doing without also asking a favor?
- ☐ Do I find myself getting annoyed or frustrated when they reach out to me needing something?
- ☐ Am I feeling like the "strong friend" who can't go to them for the same things they come to me for?

If you answered yes to these, then your friendship might be in the yellow zone. Making a conscious decision to give yourself the time and space to recalibrate and get your energy back is crucial so you don't abandon yourself and let the relationship fall into red light territory.

RED LIGHT RELATIONSHIPS

A red light relationship is *toxic*. I use that word loosely, but I'm sure you understand. In these relationships, both sides are tolerated, but neither of you really gets anything from it. It's more familiar than anything else. We see these a lot when people hang out with the same friends from high school while trying to make something new of themselves. Your friends from high school are "known"; they are comfortable and familiar, but you know there is a massive misalignment between where they are and where you want to be. Conversations seem to only exist on their energy frequency, and when you try to speak in yours, it feels as though you are all speaking different languages. They don't really hear what you're saying or see what you see in the world anymore.

Yet, you continue to stay and put even more energy into these relationships, thinking that will help them. They more than likely vent about you when you aren't around, and you definitely vent about them when they aren't around. These relationships are not safe spaces for truth or authentic expression. So, we bottle up how we feel and keep ourselves in an environment that drains us energetically. This is just another form of self-abandonment.

When we neglect our feelings and stay in relationships that make us feel small or misunderstood or even judged, we have fully abandoned ourselves. We have recalibrated our energy and are sending out a signal into the universe that says, "Bring me more of this terrible feeling." It is no surprise that we continuously find more red zone relationships. We continue to attract more people that make us feel judged, misunderstood, or like we are never good enough.

Red light relationships are dangerous. Red almost always signifies danger or that you need to stop moving forward. When we surround ourselves with relationships in the red zone, we are putting a stop to our growth and any forward momentum we had. These relationships are bottomless pits that never stop siphoning our energy.

One choice has the power to remove our ability to make any more choices for ourselves. I am almost always sure when a client of mine has entered a red zone environment because they start to see the world differently, speak differently, and act differently. The world becomes hard and unjust. They start to list all the reasons why they can't get things done. The "cruel and unjust" world constantly shows them all the reasons why they can't take the next step or that they simply have no more choices to make. The infinite abundant universe is only abundant for everyone else. Does that sound like someone who is in a green zone relationship with life? With themselves? With the universe? With God? Of course not.

Our environment is a direct reflection of our internal state. If we are attracting people who see life as unfair and scarce, it is because we see the same things. Even if we try to consciously chant affirmations in the mirror about how happy and abundant we are, it only goes so far. You are in a red light relationship with the universe if you are merely tolerating your existence within it. If you "say the right things" or "act civil" when convenient but you resort back to scarcity, envy, or resentment of others when you are alone, you will always find yourself with less.

In a red zone, you have stopped moving forward; you have stopped the flow of the universe. You are no longer able to see with a positive outlook—the more you look, the more despair you find. Life continues to prove to you how unfair it is, and you yell to the heavens asking, "WHY ME?" Remember, the universe doesn't "have it out" for us. It doesn't even know what "good" or "bad" is in context to us. It simply provides in abundance whatever it is you are asking to see more of. We ask by thinking and seeking.

Red light relationships can feel impossible to escape, especially when they are with your family. Every time you go home, you're miserable. We try to justify it. "They're my family. I have to see them. I want to keep a relationship with my family." I really wonder what your definition of family is. Mine is simple. My family is not chosen for me; my family is chosen by me. My family chooses me back and uplifts me the same way I uplift them. My family only exists in the green zone. We place a larger emphasis on bloodline than we do on energetic signature. Our blood is primal; our blood is human. Our energy and creative power are eternal. They supersede time and space. Why would we shut ourselves off from our eternal power of the infinite divine because of something as silly as blood?

I often face a counterargument based on time allocated toward the relationship.

"I can't just walk away from the family I've had for the last twenty-five years."

To which I usually respond, "How many of those years have they empowered you and fully supported your evolution?"

You see, the "family" we have in red zones and choose to keep are actually just people who have leveraged the "family" pedestal as a means to constantly abuse us. I would assume that if I were with a *chosen* family for twenty-five years, I would feel the safest, most supported, and loved I've ever been. Same concept, completely different outcomes. One path makes us a victim; the other path makes us a creator. Take a second right now and imagine if you could draw up your ideal family: how they act, what they do, how they talk to you, support you, treat you, and make you feel. Close your eyes and just feel into that desired family right now. Is that what your current "family" feels like? If not, then you do not have to feel shame or guilt for removing yourself from "family" that actively chooses not to treat you like family.

The energetic boundaries and core values you uphold for your relationships will dictate your entire experience of life. We are energetic beings, and whatever energy we allow (and we allow by tolerating) to blend into our own will be the catalyst for whatever life brings us next.

If your relationships are in the red zone, it is time to stop and reassess the environment entirely. If there is a red light in traffic and you keep driving, pretending you don't see it, you are sure to crash. You will only put your life and others at risk. You must hold yourself in integrity to what you will and will no longer tolerate in your life. One of my core values is, "If they don't make me feel good, they are not my people." My life has now been restructured around the laws of energy, and it has opened the most profound doors of blessings that I could have ever dreamed of. Energy never lies; humans do.

When I started governing my relationships, decisions, and life by the laws of energy and the universe, everything fell into place at rapid speed. It was difficult to stand up for myself and set boundaries with those who I thought were closest to me at that time. My ego would tremble when people came back with "You think you're too good for us." I was fearful that I was making the wrong decision and that everyone would hate me or think poorly of me. That was something that stopped me from making hard decisions for myself: the fear of what people would think of me. I gave that more power over what I thought of myself.

But I finally realized that my life was never going to change that way. I was stuck at a red light in rush hour traffic with no AC, no radio, and horns blaring all around me.

Here are some questions I ask myself to audit if I am in a red zone relationship or not:

- ☐ Am I tolerating this person, or do I genuinely enjoy spending time with them?
- ☐ Do I ever feel good after being around them?
- ☐ Are they constantly trying to show me how unjust the world is by their own thoughts and actions?
- ☐ Are they actively searching for growth opportunities?
- ☐ Do they think of solutions or only think of problems?
- ☐ Am I only in this relationship because it's familiar?
- ☐ What is this person providing me that is adding value to my life? And I to theirs?
- ☐ When I am around these people, does it motivate my drive or motivate my laziness?
- ☐ Are they on my same wavelength?
- ☐ Do they make me feel seen, heard, understood, and supported?

From the guy who always had struggles with relationships of any caliber his whole life, I can confidently proclaim that the day I decided to improve the quality of my relationships was the day I started improving the quality of my life and saving a lot of precious energy.

To all of the amazing people I now have relationships with, thank you. Thank you for keeping me in the green zone. It truly brings tears to my eyes feeling the immense gratitude I have for you. Thank you for loving me unconditionally, supporting me through every phase of my growth, and always telling me what I need to hear. Through all my mistakes and my humanity as I've grown, you never turned me away and also pushed me to bring the most authentic version of myself back out. You are all my rocks, and I would not be anywhere close to the position I am now in without every single one of you. I love you endlessly.

Green light.

THE PATTERN

Sure, I grew up in a trailer park with a single mother. We weren't the wealthiest people on the planet. But we still had a roof (although there were holes in it and tarps over those holes) and food in our bellies. My diet consisted dominantly of Top Ramen, bowls of cereal, and canned chili without the beans. Once a week my mom would make us our "treat dinner" of tilapia, canned green beans, and instant mashed potatoes. It was a good life. I got to play outside in the woods, sticks as swords, rocks as bombs, and trees as castles.

I lived far away from most of my friends from school, so my summers were usually spent alone. My mom had to work, so usually she would leave me next door at my grandmother's house. During seventh grade, my mom decided to try homeschooling me. I wasn't exactly a fan favorite with teachers at my school. I got into a lot of fights with other students, and the target on my back just seemed to get bigger and bigger. So that summer I was inside my trailer a lot, doing schoolwork while my mom was at work and my friends that lived at the trailer park were all outside playing. My mom had a rule that I was not allowed to go outside until she got home from work. I would sit at the window and watch as my friends played outside without me, constantly feeling helplessness, even a slight panic in my nervous system.

My mother was a bit overprotective in this regard, and although she meant well, it created some pretty deep wounds in my subconscious. I developed a pattern in my life that I would not recognize until twenty years later: I had become accustomed to watching from the outside while everyone else had fun without me. The situation subconsciously programmed me into thinking that "fun" wasn't something I was to be included in . . . until a feminine presence had "returned home," which allowed me to go outside and be "free."

Across the street from our trailer were these three larger hills that all the kids played on. Another rule from my mother was that I wasn't allowed to go past the second hill because she couldn't see me at the third. You know where all the kids always played the most? That's right, the third hill. We would all be playing *Star Wars* or *Lord of the Rings*, fighting imaginary orcs. They would all make their way to the third hill while I stood at the top watching them play and have fun without me. I unknowingly maintained that distance in all my relationships moving into adulthood. Always having some sort of gap or separation between my friends and me. It felt as though whenever my friends and I got together in a group setting, I would find myself on the outskirts, disconnected from the group as a whole.

What was also happening inside me was that my body was getting addicted to the emotions and feelings of "longing" to be with people or be included by people. Feeling imprisoned and helpless became an addiction in my physiology. Whenever I did finally get to play or formed connections in relationships later in my life, I would become disinterested rather quickly. I would start to pull away and wall myself off from deepening connections. I didn't know how to function if I didn't feel helpless and separated from people, always desperately wanting to "play" with them. The act of "wanting" to play with them became more appealing to me than actually "playing" with them.

The patterns we are addicted to will hold us back and drain our energy until we become aware of them. Awareness is the first step to repatterning.

I had developed an imprisonment pattern with any feminine presence in my life. When living with one of my past girlfriends, when she was out of the house, I would stay inside the whole time. It would feel wrong to go anywhere without her there; I would feel frantic if I were to even leave the house to do things before she got back. Looking back on it now, it makes me laugh at how confusing the situation was for all parties. My girlfriend would be gone for hours, and the second she got home, I would get a massive burst of energy and head out to do all my tasks.

"Why do you wait until right when I get home to go do things?" she would always ask.

The answer was I hadn't become aware of the pattern yet. I just always told myself I was busy, but it was a deep-rooted pattern. I needed the feminine presence as my permission to be able to be free—which turned all my intimate relationships into co-dependencies. Sure, I'd been in love while I was in that pattern, but had I ever actually known what *real* love felt or looked like? No.

Love has always been very hard for me. One of the most difficult experiences to let into my reality and accept as real.

I know how much my mother loves me. I also know that

while we all loved my grandmother and she loved us, we would joke about how grumpy she always was. My grandmother was always complaining about something, and we all loved her for it. Over my healing journey, I've been able to develop an empathic viewpoint of how unable she was to love herself. My grandma only knew how to look at the deficiencies in the world and in people. That doesn't make her bad; it just shows that she was wounded. Her mother probably only ever pointed out the things she was doing wrong and how she needed to behave in order to be accepted. That's not love; that's manipulation. If she could never give love to herself, how could she have ever given love to my mother? If it was never given to my mother, how could my mother have ever given it to herself, let alone given it to a child? A pattern begets a pattern.

I remember one summer when I was nine or ten. Our trailer park was in the middle of a campground in the mountains, and there was a public pool about two trailer rows from my grandmother's trailer. It was the middle of summer. The sun was out, and it was hot. There were a bunch of "campers" down at the pool having fun, and we could hear them inside. My grandmother threw down her newspaper and said, "Nicolas, go tell them to be quiet. They're being obnoxious."

I tried to convince her otherwise, but she shoved her pointer finger in my face and said it again. When my grandmother gave you the pointer finger, you knew you had no choice. I walked out of her gate and down to the pool to see thirty or so people having fun in the water. My grandmother was eyeing me like a hawk from her window to make sure I went all the way down. As I approached the fence, I gulped, and with my voice shaking, said, "Excuse me . . . Excuse me, everybody."

They all got quiet and looked at me. Having no idea how to pull this off and not sound insane, I decided to lie. "I was wondering if you guys could please be a little bit quieter. It's my grandma. She's very sick and tired. She is trying to nap right now."

The awkward stare of a thousand eyes commenced, and one of the older kids muttered, "Uh . . . okay, yeah, sure. We'll keep it down."

I dropped my head and ran back toward my grandma's trailer, filled with embarrassment and definitely trauma.

I spent a lot of years in my early twenties feeling resentful toward my mother and grandmother for "not loving me properly." These were complicated emotions and feelings that I did not know how to process or understand, paired with guilt for thinking I was being ungrateful for being upset and feeling neglected. I hadn't been through enough life yet to understand and see it clearly. I didn't have the awareness yet. I was imprisoned in patterns that drained my energy and only allowed me to see a black-and-white world colored by my own wounds. I didn't know what I was looking at.

If you don't understand what you're looking at, it doesn't matter what you see.

All I saw was myself as a victim, trapped in the trailer. Once I saw the pattern for what it was, I started softening and understanding my mother and grandmother a lot more. The cards just happened to fall the way that they did. There was never an intention to hurt me or to create patterns of neglect or abandonment. But they happened. The only thing to be done now is to forgive and learn to love so that we don't carry harmful patterns on to our children, friends, and relationships.

I'm very proud of the man I am today, and I have so much

love, compassion, and gratitude for my mother. I am still working to break the patterns that disempower me and drain my energy. Allowing myself the space to sit with myself, hold myself, and love myself through all the darkness is essential. Being the parent for my inner child that he needed when I was his age. I am aware of what he needs now, and I get to be the one to go back and give that to him.

I would never have been able to break into that level of awareness, empathy, and power had the journey not unfolded the way that it did. That's the beginning of acceptance, and that's what we're tackling next.

CHAPTER 3

ACCEPTANCE

We catch glimpses of it. That "best" version of ourselves.

Call it your higher self, the future you, or whatever label you need to put on it. You catch glimpses of this version coming out every once in a while, and it feels like ecstasy. When you wake up in the morning and know today is going to be an incredible day.

Everything seems to work out for you. Your coffee gets bought by a stranger, you hit every green light, you close every deal, you get a promotion, you get handed opportunities and blessings left and right. You are powerful, you feel unstoppable, and you are so assured of yourself that nobody could talk you out of this raw power you feel inside of you.

Yet, once the day is over and you go to bed, you wake up the next morning, and it's right back to square one. You go right back into your self-loathing, self-questioning, and low self-esteem and become a doormat again. You convince yourself that what you experienced was some rare phenomenon that you couldn't possibly tap into consistently.

Well, I am here to tell you that you are wrong.

Let me ask you a few questions.

When you tap into this "higher version" of yourself, I'm

willing to bet you aren't questioning whether or not you are actually yourself, are you?

That's because at that moment, during that day, you *are being yourself*. You can only ever just be you. It is impossible to be anyone else. So, how can we be two completely different versions of ourselves?

You wake up aligned because something stimulated that part of your brain first thing in the morning, and you chose to take that and paint the rest of the day in that same color. You accepted the gift within you.

The same thing happens when something stimulates you in a negative way first thing in the morning. You drop your coffee mug on the floor. As it shatters into pieces, you say, "I guess it's going to be one of those days today." Once you have claimed the day, that is the experience that will play out for you.

Your days are a choice.

You convince yourself that feeling incredible is rare. So rare, in fact, that you deny it to be possible to bring that version of yourself out full-time. Well, here is the truth: you have experienced this version of yourself because that is simply who you are. If that version wasn't actually you, then you would not be able to *be* that version in the first place. Not at all. You simply just cannot be something that you are not. You can pretend to be for a time but not for long. So, when this version of you comes out—or maybe I should say, when you *choose* to be that version of yourself—you can just as easily *choose* to remain as that individual.

In these moments of your life, when that lion or tiger in you roars and you feel its full power, know that to be the very depth of who you actually are. The magnitude of your power comes down to tapping into yourself. Acceptance is about recognizing the best in you and choosing it.

WOUNDS

It is one thing to become aware of what's really going on in your internal world. It is a whole new thing entirely to accept it. Acceptance is arguably one of the hardest things we navigate through as human beings. We are obsessed with getting "justice" and wanting people who have hurt us to suffer for causing us suffering. We can't accept someone for what they did to us; we can't accept that we have the power to change our perspective at any given point . . . it seems that the only thing we are willing to accept is more suffering for ourselves.

At age twenty-eight, I experienced the full force of what real heartbreak felt like. As I write these words, my heart continues to beat irregularly and ache like nothing I have ever felt: a fifty-pound cinder block on my chest at all times while my feet feel glued to the floor. The weight is almost too heavy to bear. Which is exactly why I must do it. One of many attempts to accept and channel my pain will be within the words you read here.

The unique opportunities pain creates for us are relentlessly brutal and almost impossible to understand. But the opportunities lie beyond our suffering—therefore, the only way to receive them is through the pain.

As human beings, we have an innate desire to run from pain. We avoid, we lie, we deflect, and we distract ourselves with whatever we find first. It is much softer on us short-term if we put our attention elsewhere and ignore the emotions that, eventually, will have to be processed and felt in their entirety.

This notion, in itself, is horrifying. The underlying knowledge that eventually suffering will make its way into our hearts. Yet accepting our pain, our suffering, is the only way we can truly find salvation beyond it. That pain changes you at a cellular level when you choose to face it, when you choose to honor it, when you choose to accept it.

It can be very easy for life to feel like a continuous compilation of lessons taught the hard way, with pain and regret. We find it easy to claim our "demons" because it allows us to deflect our actions onto something outside of ourselves.

"That person has demons," we say. But we all do.

"That person has darkness," we say. But we all do.

We never kill our demons; we just need to learn to live beside them. Assuming anything other than this fact is extremely dangerous. Why? Because every demon, darkness, or person that you have been, every single version of you, still lives inside you. Each of them is trying to fight its way back up to get its hand on the steering wheel. Just because you have been wounded does not mean you give up and let them take back control.

A wound is evidence that you have been hurt. A scar is a testimony that you have been healed. By healing our wounds, we receive wisdom in the form of scars. Your scars are the gateway to changing the world and helping others around you, but only when you fully accept the role they were meant to play in your life. This is where we develop what some call *wisdom*. We say, "Wow, they are so wise; that must be amazing." What we fail to understand is that wisdom comes from accepting, enduring, and overcoming pain . . . a lot of it. My good friend John Romaniello said, "Wisdom is learning the lesson you need after you've already needed it."

We begin to change the world when we finally decide to lead with our scars.

YOUR MISSION

That's the rough side of acceptance. There is a more exciting side too: a surrender to your life's mission.

What were you put on this earth to do? Do you know? I am not asking if you are successful, rich, or even happy. I am asking if you know why you are here. What your assignment really is.

I have worked with copious amounts of high-level athletes, entrepreneurs, and elite individuals with my time here so far. What I have found more often than not is that we lose ourselves in the façade of material success. We attach our value and our metric of happiness to what we have in our bank account, what car we drive, what clothes we wear, etc. If an individual has all of these boxes checked off, it can be very difficult to unravel their constrained view of reality and show them they are actually in the wrong place.

Now I want to be clear, there is nothing wrong with living this lifestyle. There is nothing wrong with making millions of dollars doing something you are pretty good at and living a life of self-orientation. This life was meant to be experienced in whatever way we *choose* to experience it; I have no judgment on you if you *choose* to live your life for yourself only. But you should put down this book and move onward.

Who I am speaking to are the ones who know deep down that there is still something missing . . . but you can't quite put your finger on it.

Back when I was twenty-seven and living in Houston, I was at the most miserable point in my life. My business was booming because it was my distraction from the harsh reality of the life that I was a prisoner to. My ego loved to boast about how incredible of a fitness coach I was—we had almost fifty athletes compete in bodybuilding that year, and every single one walked away with a trophy. I was doing about $200k a month at this time . . . and I hated every second of it.

But hey, I was the man, I was making incredible money, and I was good at what I was doing. Obviously, this was what I was put here to do—or so I convinced myself.

By chasing an endless thirst that could never be quenched, I lost myself to the rat race. I bought a $220,000 Acura NSX (which I LOVED) to give me some sort of dopamine hit or happiness to validate that I was successful. Short-lived ecstasy. I returned it six months later because I was already "over it." I was empty.

The reason I was constantly chasing external stimuli was because internally I knew that something was missing. I knew that there was a puzzle piece that wasn't properly in place, and I was just banging it with my fist trying to get it to fit so I could get the job done.

For men especially, it can be very hard not to tie your sense of self-confidence, self-worth, and even happiness to your material success. Nowadays, most men and women would rather be envied for their material success than be respected for their character. We just run around wounded, searching for anything we can to show our status and prove our superiority to others.

There has to be something more than just money, right? If I couldn't find happiness making almost $7,000 a day, did happiness even exist on this path? The answer is: absolutely the fuck not. I became obsessed with a destination, and I hyper-fixated on thoughts like, "When I get to X, then I will experience Y." All of my power had been pushed outside of me. Nothing left inside except an empty space, desperate to be filled.

The man who loves to walk will go farther than the man who

loves the destination. The truth was that I hated walking. Not because of the walking itself but because of who I was while I walked. When we know something is missing and we continue to stay in the same position out of fear or a false sense of security, we start to unravel one conscious strand at a time. There is nowhere more dangerous than a situation you are not supposed to be in. So inevitably, my entire life imploded.

After a few dark nights of the soul and almost a full year of nervous system regulation paired with endless hours of subconscious rewiring, I was able to accept the reality that I wasn't fulfilling my purpose and break away from this "matrix" a lot of us get stuck in for our entire lives.

For once in my life, I was able to stop running, stop chasing a high, stop seeking validation, stop fleeing my demons. I finally just stopped and sat, allowing all of my lessons, traumas, pain, sadness, regret, guilt, and all the other fun stuff to finally catch up. I said enough was enough, and I turned around with my feet planted and braced for impact. The more I stayed in the storm and allowed myself to finally process everything (even things from my childhood I had brushed off as no big deal), my entire reality changed. Everything I used to see no longer looked the same. I saw problems and holes that needed to be filled in the world and finally could hear myself think. I could finally hear God give instruction because my cluttered headspace was starting to clear out. The more I processed, the more I accepted, and the clearer I saw.

I have to give another dedication in this book to Annie. Had she not had the strength and discernment to know that we needed to go our own separate ways in order to grow, I would have nothing right now. I would still be playing the same games, running the same tracks, and facing the same struggles. She mirrored back to me everything I needed to work on and inspired me to finally stop and go all in on my healing journey.

So, as I finally stopped to face the beast (myself), I realized my entire life had been built on a façade: "I'm good at what I do. Therefore, it is what I am meant to do."

Don't get me wrong, I absolutely love(d) fitness coaching and my athletes. We built such an incredible family that got me through some of the toughest times in my life. I always prided myself on the way I coached. I just did it differently. I put an immense emphasis on leadership development, incorporating the spiritual side of things, aligning people in every aspect of their lives. I spent my entire life as an entrepreneur empowering people to be the best versions of themselves and never realized that I was using "fitness coaching" as a container to put it inside of.

I always told myself, "I'm a fitness coach who works this way," but what I had to accept was that I actually just . . . worked that way. And also did fitness coaching. I looked at all the people I had helped, all the other leaders I had played even a fractional role in progressing, and I noticed that all of them were just absolutely dominating their lives after "graduating" from working with me. It got me insanely hyped up.

It lit me up more than anything else I had experienced to that point in my life. Once I started allowing myself the possibility of another scenario of who the fuck I was and what my assignment actually was here in this lifetime, all of those situations took on a new hue. It became a memory that supercharged my motivation to keep pushing forward.

PERSPECTIVE EMPOWERMENT

I have been called a Perspective Empowerment Coach by a few of the individuals I work with, and I will say it's got a nice ring to it. But what exactly is perspective empowerment, and how can we use it to accept and surrender to our life mission?

The way we view the world has an immense impact on how we go about trying to change it. It may even push us away from wanting to change it at all. Let's talk about the brain for a second so we can understand a bit more about how we truly perceive reality.

The subconscious brain is insanely powerful. It takes in roughly 127 million bits of information per second, while our conscious brain only takes in about eight. If we were consciously aware of all of the stimuli around us at all times, we would fall into a manic episode and never come back. The brain has developed a very smooth way of prioritizing what matters and what doesn't.

If you are sitting inside reading this right now, is your air conditioner on? Or maybe a fan? Did you hear it at all until you read that line? Maybe it wasn't your AC but something else. My point is that because you were not focusing on that sound, your brain deemed it unimportant and deleted it from your conscious viewpoint.

Our perception of reality is really just a projection of what is going on inside of us. We filter reality with a multitude of lenses: memory, identity, core values, belief, meta programs, time, location, etc. When we take in bits of information, the brain has three main jobs: delete, distort, and generalize.

Because of our filters, the reality we perceive is only about 0.006 percent of what is actually going on in the real world. The main takeaway from this is that our reality is subjective. It is personal and subject to our own thoughts and beliefs.

If our reality is subjective, then our reality can be changed.

This can be our greatest tool or our greatest handicap. Just because we have the power to change our own reality does not mean we have the power to change anybody else's. But by making the decision to change your own reality, you have the opportunity to become an inspiration for other people to *choose* a change in theirs. It has to be their choice every single time.

So, how does this tie into perspective empowerment?

Well, when we water down perspective, we see that perspective is just made up from belief systems. A belief system cannot be destroyed; it can only be transformed. I used to believe that God was not the absolute and that it was only the universe that we could speak to. Until I went to an all-men's church retreat and heard God speak directly to me . . . but more on that later. The point here is that if I didn't necessarily believe in God, I wasn't going to just randomly start believing. Something needed to come in to transform my current belief into a new belief.

For children, they believe Santa is real until they catch their mom tiptoeing through the trailer to put the presents under the tree as you watch from the top of your bunk bed and then roll over to cry yourself to sleep . . . I would assume . . . because I never experienced that personally.

Anyway, a belief must be presented with opposition for it to leap to in order to change. This is where our egos can become very destructive to our life's purpose. When the only story we know is that we are not meant for greatness, when greatness shows up, we will never believe that it is actually for us. We will sit on the sidelines without taking action. Why would you act on an opportunity you don't believe is meant for you? Are you starting to see how your perspective on life will dictate how you go about changing the world? And therefore, how the acceptance of your potential can transform everything?

Waking up to your life's purpose is turbulent. It is the farthest thing from a smooth or comfortable ride. It is really fucking hard. The reality you knew starts to melt away, everything that used to matter to you no longer does, and you are beyond overwhelmed with the dreams and visions that keep popping up in your head.

We all have dreams; we all *see* a life of "unimaginable" possibilities—yet we think it's not possible. How can you see a future that's not supposed to be yours? How can you imagine something and say it's unimaginable? When we actually pop the hood and look at the inner workings of our limiting beliefs, we will more often than not see that they are held together by duct tape and chewing gum. It is the fact that we are too afraid to pop the hood that allows these fragile, misleading beliefs to run our entire lives as we sit back and damn ourselves for always "self-sabotaging."

This life you keep thinking about? That one you see when you close your eyes? It is there, and it is waiting for you.

Can you imagine what your life would feel like if you woke up every day knowing you were doing exactly what you were put here to do? Would you feel different? Would you walk differently? How would your energy levels be? Remember the Asleep chapter . . . remember the Pattern—we keep ourselves imprisoned in a cycle of energy-draining mundanity because we do not believe another option exists. We drain our energy, and we are forced to play small because we are terrified of our true power. Terrified of playing big.

My job is to trigger you. My message is meant to be polarizing and trigger people into an evolution. A lot of people take offense when you are speaking truth into the depths of their souls and wounds. The truth will make people lash out if they are living within their own dysfunction.

Good.

You need to wake up to what is really yours in this life. You need to awaken to your life's purpose. You need to start surrounding yourself with the people who see what is inside of you and who honor it instead of fear it. You need to stop bullshitting yourself with the same stories that have held you stagnant your entire life. Instead of slowly inching forward, it's time for you to get a running start and leap. Asleep to Aware to Accepting.

That's what we do. That is the entire backbone of our Impakt Legacy Mastermind. Helping you remember who the fuck you are and what you were put here to do and building you up into that leader role so you can go make your own impact in this world. Conscious leadership is what will change this world for the better.

Your life purpose is here. It is slamming its fists on the door so loud you can no longer avoid it. You either open the door or it will knock the door down. By surrendering to your life's purpose, you also break all the chains from your past that have been convincing you that you're meant for nothing.

It is time for you to come back home to yourself and push forward. Your strength may tell you no, but the path still demands yes. It will demand sacrifice, it will demand stress, it will demand moving mountains and slaying giants. It will take everything that you have inside of you to push into this life you know is meant for you.

The only way you will be able to get there is if you surrender yourself to the anointing placed upon your life and accept that all the pain you've been through has only prepared you to embrace your own inevitable greatness.

NEVER ACCEPTING DEFEAT: MR. STAN

There is one thing you are never permitted to accept: defeat.

During my time training at 214 Fitness (more on that in Chapter 7), an elderly couple walked into the gym one day. Ann and Stan. Ann was looking for some help with her husband. She wheeled him in and explained that Stan had suffered from a stroke down the center of his spine, negatively affecting both sides of his body. Stan had served in combat, and I could tell just from the few words he could barely get out that he was one hell of a soldier. Ann explained to me that the doctors said he would basically be helpless for the rest of his life; there was no real way of helping him improve. From my personal experience with doctors, this is a very common thing to hear.

She asked if I was comfortable giving it a try to see what it could produce and if we could help him get in some better shape and improve his coordination. I had to confess to her that I did not feel qualified for the job. She looked me in my eyes and said, "We just need someone who won't give up on him."

That I can do.

I spent the first few sessions with Mr. Stan assessing his barriers of coordination, strength, stability, and body awareness. He was unable to walk due to the stroke, so we did all of this from his wheelchair. I could tell Stan was a fighter. Even through all the pain and burning, he would always crack jokes and leave us both laughing. Eventually we started getting more comfortable, and he trusted me with pushing him a bit harder. For about four to five weeks of seeing Stan, I was hugging my arms around him in the wheelchair and standing him up and putting him back down over and over and over.

I would put a tiny little step next to his chair and have him work on picking one foot up, just to see if he could even get a foot on top of the step and back down. This was very challenging for him; it took most of his strength just to lift his foot a few times. As we continued to work together, we kept our hearts light and our energy high. Stan began to improve on all markers.

Then one day Stan and Ann were late for his sessions. They were never late. Being a military man, Stan was always punctual. I began to get a little worried that something might have happened to him as the clock went five minutes past noon, then ten, then fifteen.

Did I push him too hard, and he tried to do something on his own? Did he try to stand up and fall? My thoughts started spiraling. *Maybe I shouldn't have agreed to try and help him. Maybe I was instilling a far-fetched belief in him that he could get his function back at his age. Maybe the doctors were right. I never should have done this.*

The doors finally opened, and I was amazed to see Mr. Stan walking into my gym with the help of a push walker and the biggest smile on his face to show me the improvements he had been making. That remains one of my favorite memories and damn sure one of the most inspiring. Stan was not a fully functional man on his own and never would be again; he still needed help standing up and sitting down, but he was now able to fully walk on his own with the help of his walker, and he had such a higher energy to him. We started ramping up our efforts and weight-loading his walker to have him push forward with weight in order to build back some lost muscle from the wheelchair use. Stan would push about a hundred and twenty pounds up and down the gym parking lot by the time I was done at 214 Fitness. He and Ann did not live in the state, so they would make a yearly visit. Every time they were in town, he made sure to get on my calendar. At my own facility, NK Fitness, we saw Stan get to standing up and sitting down using his own legs and just holding onto a TRX attachment we had hooked up to the rigs. We played catch with a large stability ball to improve his coordination and did anything else we could think of for him to work and still have fun.

I can't help but think about Stan whenever I feel helpless in my life now. Stan was handed the ultimate excuse to give up: a diagnosis from a doctor. Most people choose to personally identify with a given diagnosis and allow it to control their entire lives. Not Stan. We live in a world now where people have forgotten how to ask questions and think for themselves. We are being conditioned for the government and anyone else in "authority" to think for us so we have an excuse to remain unconscious in our lives.

Stan decided to ask one simple question that turned his entire life around even when every odd said it wasn't possible: What if I could?

We are not destined to sit back and watch ourselves rot as our lives pass us by. That's why we have so many people unmotivated, depressed, anxious, and overwhelmed. There is a voice deep inside all of us saying, "What the fuck are you doing? GET UP." This isn't how we are meant to live. We were born with the ability to push our natural boundaries.

Human beings are fascinating creatures. We are the only species that willingly self-harms. We are the only species that willingly harms the planet. We are the only species with both a soul and an ego.

Yet, we are also the only species that has the ability to perform *supernaturally*. No other animal species on this planet possesses that superpower. Lions will always be lions, and wolves will always be wolves, but humans have proven time and time again that limitations do not exist for us. We have been shown that living a "natural" life leaves most of us feeling unfulfilled and yearning for more. I believe this is because we know deep down that we are living beneath what our full potential can be. I believe that in order for us to perform *supernaturally,* we have to stop closing ourselves off from the supernatural. I believe that spirituality is the key to unlocking the doors of our truest potential.

Show me a person imprisoned by thinking through the constraints of natural ability in this world, and I will show you a person walking backwards on the path of life. I will show you a person wondering why others seem to keep getting so far ahead as they continue to roll around in the lower consciousness level thoughts and emotions of shame, guilt, envy, victimhood, etc. I will show you a person whose favorite catchphrase is "must be nice."

Can you imagine what Stan's life would look like if he chose to sit in that wheelchair and cast envy and hate toward everyone he saw walking the way he used to? He never would have come into the gym, he never would have pushed when everything said it was pointless, he never would have gotten even a small percentage of his life back if he had just listened and never asked questions about what he was capable of. Stan fought with everything he had to even make a 0.4 percent improvement in his apparently helpless situation. Most people throw in the towel just seeing the scale go up two pounds after a week of eating better.

Our world is now designed to keep you playing small. It is designed to keep you second-guessing yourself and stuck in the child archetype, waiting for someone to tell you what to do and how to think. All I ask you to do before you give in to your circumstances and think your life has been sentenced is, "What if I could?"

What if you could lose the weight, kick the addiction, start that business, make the money, buy the car, overcome depression, heal yourself, take the vacation, marry the person, or live that life? What if you could? And what if you could do it regardless of what anybody else says or what has been "proven" can and can't be done?

Why can't you be the next person to prove our broken system wrong and help start the mending of our collective wounds? Why can't you be the person who steps up and defies the odds? If Mr. Stan can do it, what if you could too?

I think we are all waiting for our miraculous hero's story to just "happen." Sitting around as an observer of our lives, praying for the time when everything will magically shift in our favor and provide us the fruits from the labors we have never performed. As I am sure you have gathered if you've made it this far, I almost didn't make it. Not only did I almost not make it, but I also almost didn't make it multiple times. Yet, for some reason, I did.

It is normal to think that maybe whoever wrote the book we are reading might have more authority or have a bigger, more grandiose story than we do. That's a trick being played on us by our lower selves. I am willing to bet that you have also been through something in your life that you almost didn't make it through. I am certain that you have had to slay many giants who stood before you in your life in order to get to this point. I think you are an absolute inspiration to be able to sit here reading this book at your leisure after everything you have gone through.

Paradoxically, we seem to cling to this one notion that haunts us indefinitely: the notion that we aren't going to make it through whatever giant currently stands before us or whatever giant may be on its way. When you have irrefutable evidence that you have yet to be defeated in your life thus far. You have been beaten, you have wanted to give up, you may have wanted to end your life like I once did—and then you didn't. You pushed through. I know how incredibly hard that can be to do. I also know how much courage and strength it takes to keep moving forward after experiencing pain, loss, embarrassment, hate, etc. We hold a delicate world in our hands, and there are lowlifes everywhere who wish to keep you from pushing higher. You are not alone.

It would make you sick to your stomach if you saw the number of brilliant individuals I work with who have greatness in them but are completely paralyzed from pursuing their dreams by the fear of being harshly ridiculed by society. Have you ever read of a single person doing monumental things in their lives who didn't have people who tried to tear them down and misunderstand them? That story doesn't exist.

I think those lowlife trolls should be ashamed of themselves for being so filled with judgment and hatred that they put out some people's fire before they even get started. They are so filled with hate that people fear even trying to become who they were meant to be out of the fear of harshness. It is an absolute tragedy that these people cannot focus enough on themselves to empower others in seeking their greatness.

That said, as we covered in the chapter on acceptance, everyone has a role to play in this world. If there were never people who wanted to see you fail, who cast stones at every belief and thought you had and tried to sabotage your success, we would never have the hero's journey. There need to be giants to slay and demons to battle in order to fortify you with the strength necessary to change the world in your own way. I personally seek them out and give them a voice on my platforms. I take their hateful questions and post them publicly with an answer in hopes of showing other aspiring fighters just how weak these lowlifes are and how little their words can affect us.

People's power over you can only be measured by the extent of the power you choose to give to them. If you give them no power, they have no power. They are energy suckers, and you have so much greatness inside of you that they can't help but feed on it. It shows them where they are lacking, so they are desperate to try and pull down your greatness in hopes that it will fill them up instead. These people need help and will hopefully get it eventually.

For now, they are not meant to be your concern. I need you to focus on your purpose.

You may notice that this chapter is a little shorter. That's because the distance between Awareness and Awakening is a transition as quick as saying yes or no. Once you have woken up and recognized the good and the bad in your life, I urge you to say yes. Accept your struggles for the lessons they taught you and accept your dreams as reality. And then buckle up. You're about to start seeing things you've never seen before.

ACCEPTANCE TASK #1

If you are listening to the audiobook, I recommend waiting on this section until you have time to sit down, as I will be guiding you through a meditation.

I want you to think about a story you are still holding onto. I want you to see the face of the person who hurt you the most. Maybe it was a parent, a partner, a friend, or an abuser. See their face.

I want you to write down who hurt you, how they hurt you, and how old you were when this incident happened. Maybe it was last week, maybe it was when you were six. You can do this exercise as many times as you need to if more than one person has hurt you. For now, just focus on the first one that comes up, as that is the one taking the majority of your energy right now.

Once you're done, I am going to ask you to go into a meditation. You don't have to be a seasoned meditation veteran for this exercise to work.

Go sit down in a quiet room by yourself and close your eyes. Take a deep breath in through your nose, all the way into your belly, then up through your chest. Hold for five seconds at the top, then slowly let it all fall out through your mouth. Repeat these breaths for five rounds. Each time you let your breath out, you will allow yourself to shift slowly back into the memory of the incident that hurt you. Allow yourself to float into your body of that timeframe . . . see what you saw, hear what you heard, feel what you felt.

You may notice some very intense emotions or sensations in your body as your consciousness begins to re-experience this event. Keep breathing consistently into that sensation while reciting this mantra in your head: "I am completely here with you right now."

What we are doing is reconnecting with the younger version of yourself and allowing them to make their way back to the surface. They've been buried down with all your other emotions for so long that they may feel you've abandoned them. Our hurt selves need us more than ever, and when we avoid painful emotions by distracting ourselves whenever they arise, we are abandoning the version of ourselves asking for love.

Once you are here and the body is really worked up emotionally, I want you to allow your memory to re-experience that event as you observe it from a third-person viewpoint. Look at the event as an observer and see that younger version of you. Walk in between your younger self and the person who hurt them. Once there, I want you to get eye level with your younger self and gaze deeply into their eyes.

What do you see in their eyes? Is it pain? Helplessness? Sadness? Fear?

Stare even deeper. Notice how you begin to see yourself in them as they begin to see themselves in you. What we are doing here is energetically connecting to that version of yourself. Feel what they feel while they feel what you feel. One mind, one heart, one soul.

Holding the gaze with them, I want you to repeat the following phrases out loud as many times as you feel you need to until you feel the switch. You will feel it when it happens.

> I love you.
> I'm sorry.
> I love you.
> I'm sorry.
> You're safe now.
> I love you.
> I will never leave you again.
> I'm sorry.

Let the younger you feel you in your words; let them feel your heart and your love. When you feel the connection is at its strongest, I want you to hug them into your chest and allow your hearts to fully merge. We are shifting the emotional makeup of this memory and inserting love where it was lacking.

As you leave this memory to come back to the room, you can look at your younger self knowing that they are always with you, while they know you are always with them. You can talk and visit with each other whenever you please. Accept that part of you again with love. Accept that you do not need the abuser's participation for your healing to occur. Accept that the power of love that heals is the power inside of you. We must accept that the only person who is able to give every version of us what we truly need is ourselves. You are the hero you've been waiting for.

ACCEPTANCE TASK #2:

Take another sheet of paper and draw a line down the middle. On one side, write "bad things that have happened to me." On the other, write "good things that have happened to me."

Once you have your lists written out, take all the good things and rewrite them, trying to make them feel as negative as possible.

Here's an example.

Good thing that happened: I just bought the car I've always wanted.

POSITIVE LENS:

- I bought my dream car and feel so accomplished!
- It was one of the biggest goals I had for myself.
- My quality of life has improved because I feel happy every time I drive the car.
- Now it's time for me to achieve my next goal.
- I'm so happy I made this purchase because it is a testament to how well I am serving the world.

NEGATIVE LENS:

- I just bought this car, and now I have the most expensive car payment I've ever had to make.
- I could have used my money on a smarter investment, but now I'm in more debt.
- The cost of maintenance and insurance is higher now.
- Now I have to buy premium gas.
- This was the worst decision I could have made. I was not thinking smart at all.
- I'm so stupid. I'm not good with my money at all. Why do I blow my money on stupid things I don't need?

Now what's interesting about this is that some of you will resonate more with the positive lens and others with the negative. One of those realities will feel more "home" for you than the other. For now, just take note of which one it is and observe that about yourself.

What we are doing here is training the muscle in your consciousness to shift energy from one reality to another. The same event is happening in the negative lens as in the positive lens, so what's the difference? The observer. The energy we choose to place in an event will dictate its effects on our reality. If we only feel good when money comes in, but we don't choose to feel the same when money goes out, we have a poor relationship with money. We feel bad about it—and it is impossible to feel bad about something and also have it.

Let's move into a perceived "bad" thing that has happened to you.

Bad thing that happened: Your father abandoned you as a child.

NEGATIVE LENS:

- I am unworthy of my father's love.
- I am unworthy of anyone's love.
- My life is hard because I only have one parent.
- People don't know what it's like to go through what I've gone through.
- I'm angry. My father is a coward. He's a piece of shit.
- I hate my father, and I will never be anything like him. (Remember, when we hate something, we will it into existence.)
- I never had a dad to help me learn to become a man.
- I can't hold a relationship because I never observed a healthy relationship growing up.

POSITIVE LENS:

- I really am proud of the man I turned into without the guidance of a father. I never would have been this version of me had things been different.
- I am fortunate to have never had the looming need to live up to another man's expectations. I've lived my entire life free from the chains of hoping I can make my father proud of me.
- I have developed immense empathy due to all the pain and anger I used to carry.

My father must have been terrified that he wasn't ready to

raise a kid. I can't imagine how hard it must have been knowing he had a son but not having the courage to see him.

I feel so empowered now that I've learned the hard way how to be a man. The lessons feel more integrated after all the fuckups and pain. I have developed an immense sense of intuition and discernment that I would not have been able to develop otherwise.

It isn't about what happened to you. It is about which lens you use to view what happened to you. There is a reason two people can experience the same event and have two completely different outcomes. Why two sisters can grow up sexually abused by family members, and one goes on to change the world while the other spends her life seeking validation and love through sex. Why two brothers can grow up physically abused, and one goes on to rescue children from abusive households while the other spends the rest of his life getting into bar fights. Why one child becomes addicted to drugs while the other becomes a doctor, though they both experienced the same drug-addicted mother.

Acceptance comes before forgiveness, but they are one in the same. To forgive is to accept, and to accept is to forgive.

Have you ever taken a second to ask, "Why me?" in an empowering tone?

Why you? Why are you the one who can go through everything that you've been through and still be standing here with an open heart and a willingness to serve the world? How is it possible for a human to go through what you've been through and still lead with love and compassion? It's because there is something inside of you that is ready to be unlocked. The real you is waiting for you to accept and forgive so you can let go of everything that is blocking the connection to the divine.

ACCEPTANCE TASK #3:

I recommend doing this exercise before bed so you can process during sleep and wake up feeling new.

You will need a pen, a journal, and a mirror. Preferably, you are in a safe space, fully alone.

Go back to Task #1, where we relived the memory of your younger self being hurt.

Sit in meditation and feel back into that memory again. Let the emotional charge run its course through your body.

This time, instead of looking at the memory from third person, you are going to look at it in the first person. You are going to see these emotions as if you are that younger version of you.

This full meditation process should take about 5–10 minutes. If it takes a little bit longer, that's okay. We are in no rush.

Once you feel your younger self fully present on the surface, you are going to allow them to pick up the pen, open the journal, and write a letter to the person that hurt them. The most important part of this exercise is to not exercise judgment for anything that comes up or gets written. You are simply holding space for the younger version of you to finally be able to express themselves fully.

The letter can start with *Dear* ____. From there, allow the younger version of you to write anything and everything they want to say but haven't been able to express safely.

There are no rules in this. Your younger self is probably messy with their thoughts. This letter may range from "you were supposed to love me, and you didn't" to writing "fuck you" eighteen times in a row. Your only job is to hold space and let your younger self release everything they've been holding onto. Let them write as long as they need to, as angry as they desire, and as messy as it has to be.

Once they have finished, you are going to finish the letter with "... and I forgive you." You will continue to write "I forgive you" over and over until you feel the shift. You *will* feel it. Some of my clients feel it on the fifth; others have felt it on the eighty-second. Remember, no judgment—only observation.

Once you have felt *the shift*, we get to the hard part.

Walk over to your bathroom mirror and stare at yourself in the left eye. Hold this gaze for three to five minutes. It is not abnormal for your face to start morphing into someone else's. I've had clients experience seeing their face morph into their younger selves and even into the person that hurt them. Once this has been completed, you will read the full letter aloud to your reflection, letting your younger self do the reading and honoring any emotions that come up. Maybe you scream one of the *fuck you*s and then whimper another. The only thing that matters is that you remove all judgment and fully surrender to the experience. Let the tears flow and the anger be expressed. Every emotion that flows externally is no longer being held internally. You can scream, you can cry, you can whisper—all of it.

Make sure you read every single "I forgive you" aloud as well. Once you have read the letter, give yourself a little bit of time to finish processing any of the emotions that are still making their way through you. Stare back at your reflection as you process. Hold space for the version of you who has felt unseen for so long.

When you start to regulate and feel light again, you will take the letter and (safely) set it on fire. Watch it as it burns and allow any existing anger or shame to release with it. Our subconscious is extremely symbolic, and fire is associated with rebirth—burning down the old constructs of self so that the new us may rise from the ashes. This is exactly why I prefer this exercise be done right before bed, so you can rest in the lightness of energetic release and rise in the morning as a new self.

It is not uncommon to feel exhausted after these exercises. You are releasing a lot of energy that your body has learned to operate on. When we remove that dark energy, there is an emptiness of space. Feeling drained is normal as we start filling ourselves back up with fresh, clean energy again.

To accept is to forgive, and to forgive is to accept. To do both is to let go, and to let go is to surrender to a higher purpose in your life.

CHAPTER 4

AWAKENING

Life seems so simple, so why does it continue to fuck our shit up every other day? Maybe we are missing the point entirely by trying to avoid mistakes, avoid pain, and keep our lives "simple."

When we identify life in "simple" terms, it tends to enable a wide range of immensely harsh judgments on those around us and even on ourselves. Right and wrong are concepts we all know to our cores. What we perceive as right is right. What we perceive as wrong is wrong.

Yet, what if the opposite were true? What if there really was no such thing as a simple right or wrong? Why does it have to be an "or" in the first place? Right *and* wrong seems to make more sense to me.

When we can see both the right and wrong in every scenario, we start to see things through a much clearer lens—and take an unbiased view of the world and those within it. We all tend to paint the world and other people with a color that distracts us from the colors we hate seeing in ourselves. Our goal in awakening is to remove the filter and try to see things, situations, and people for what they actually are.

The truth is, our perception of the world is made up of illusions. Reality is nothing but your nervous system taking its own educated guesses at the stimulus around you and sending signals to the brain. Remember the game Telephone in preschool? Do you think it is reasonable to assume that every single one of us is hearing the same exact message with our billions of different nervous systems? Give yourself (and other people) a break. We are all here trying to figure it out as we go through it.

In the same way, the ideas and thoughts that come to you are not actually yours. The information is coming from a higher source that has chosen you as the entry portal to communicate it into the world. If you do not relay the information, it will be passed on to the next person until someone finally surrenders and allows the information to pass through them as intended.

It is not your idea; do not invite judgment of yourself based on other people's interpretation of it. If it is a terrible idea, it wasn't yours to begin with. If it ends up being a life-changing idea . . . it still wasn't yours. Awakening to this level of perception allows you to stop judging yourself and stay grounded.

You are merely a portal for information to flow through. You need to honor that.

Have you ever had a unique idea come to you, you choose to do nothing, and then three months later you see somebody bringing your idea to life? You sit there pondering how they "stole" it. Don't be a fool. The information was merely moved to another portal so it could make its way into this world. Nothing is being sent to you by accident.

SEASONS OF CHANGE

Dieter Uchtdorf said, "The thing about truth is that it exists beyond belief. It exists even if nobody believes it."

So, why do we have such a hard time speaking about what

we perceive to be our own truth? Because our ego attaches a sense of self-identity to the words we speak. We receive it as a personal attack on our character if the words are not met with praise and honor.

Some concepts and ideas only come to us as a seed. These are the larger ones, the life-changing ones. They do not blossom overnight; therefore, it is up to us to recognize them and plant and water them in order to one day reap the full harvest. The day it all clicks.

Life is nothing but a constant seasonal change between sowing and reaping. Plant and harvest. Every word and action you make today will plant a seed that you will eventually have to harvest in your future. You continue to speak negative words; you continue to reap a negative harvest. You start speaking positive words; you will reap a much different harvest next time around.

I have been humbled by life many times thus far. What I have come to find is that life will continue to keep you reliving the same painful lesson over and over again until you finally further your consciousness and find the power to break the cycle. Maybe the same financial loss repeats itself every two years; maybe you end up dating the same exact person over and over, just with a different face. "Why does this always happen to me?" we ask—and position ourselves in a helpless victim mentality. From here, the only creation we may produce is more misery. Sometimes we plant seeds that are blatantly toxic for us; we just have no idea. We're past that now. It's time to awaken.

We have to turn our focus to where it actually matters, back into ourselves. Notice the phrasing: *into* not *toward*. This is purposeful. These cycles all stem from the seeds we have planted within ourselves.

We want the life we've been manifesting to show up and knock on our door because we deserve it. What exactly does deserving mean in the first place? The definition of deserving is *worthy of being treated in a particular way, typically of being given assistance.* So, to break this down, we must first be worthy—but by whose standards? We must then be given assistance—but given by whom? God wants you to level up. The universe wants you to get out of your own way. But it has to be your choice. You need to give them something to work with other than self-loathing and fruitless comparisons with others.

Until what you currently have in front of you starts getting your full attention and you start producing results, you will not be trusted to handle more. Awaken to what's right before your eyes. Sometimes it's an opportunity. Sometimes it's a problem with self that needs work. Can God trust you with what it is you are currently asking to receive?

FEMININE WOUNDS

This is going to get personal, but I want you to understand that once you've accepted that you have some issues to sort out, you're going to awaken to some realities you might not be expecting.

It has taken me a long time to heal my wounds with the feminine. It's still an ongoing process for me as I write these pages. Always needing a presence in order to have permission to live life. How interesting of a cycle that was to observe in myself over the last decade. Seeing how I always kept myself on the outer perimeter of my friend groups to secure my own loneliness while also hoping that someone would care enough to notice and come include me. The human mind is fascinating when we observe it from a place of curiosity and love. I am so blessed to have the friend group that I have now. I have lost some of the deepest friendships I've ever had because I simply didn't know how not to be in turmoil. Bringing my problems to them (mostly my friends who were women) because I subconsciously needed a woman to think for me and tell me what to do or give me permission. Man, I might as well have had "mother wound" tattooed on my forehead!

I always had a much easier time being friends and connecting with girls growing up. I was raised by mostly women; the only male role model I had in my life was my uncle Rick, who I would only see when we all went over for dinner once a month or so. Uncle Rick was the closest thing I had to a father growing up, and he was an incredible man. He ran a ranch and knew how to fix everything from cars to light bulbs. He would always make sure to be home for lunch in time to watch his favorite soap opera, *Days of Our Lives* (I think that's what it was). He was hysterical, grounded, and kind. So generous and warm.

Beyond that, I didn't really have masculine leadership. My mom had a bunch of girlfriends who all had daughters, so when they hung out, we hung out. My mom would tell the girls to dress me up as a girl, put makeup on me, and everyone would laugh and take pictures. I started to learn that this was what I needed to do in order to be accepted. "Okay, this is making them laugh. My mom is telling me how cool it is that I'm cool with being girly and not caring. So, I guess that's what I need to keep doing."

One year I even went to school dressed up as a girl for Halloween. Dress, heels, makeup, wig, everything. My teachers were in disgust, and my peers made fun of me and picked fights with me (yes, I fought in a dress . . . and won). My mom would just tell me how insecure they all were and that I was so cool for not caring at all. For a long time, I was shown that the way I had value or received praise was by being hyperfeminine.

My friends and I at the time were in a big *Jackass* phase because of the movies and shows. Watching Steve-O dress up as a fairy and screw with people in public would have us laughing for hours. So, my friends and I would do funny little pranks and skits like that around town, during recess, whenever we could.

I learned that I was only accepted by the feminine (mom) if I was fully feminine. This programming became catastrophic later on in my early relationships. I simply did not know what it meant to be masculine. I was extremely passive with men. I never felt comfortable around them, I was always intimidated by them, and I felt inferior to any man that was around. So, I had no choice but to stick to what I knew was accepted, being hyper-feminine. I was always perceived as the "gay" kid growing up because I hung out with all the girls and let them dress me up.

MASCULINE ABSENCE

I have a father; his name is David. I did not have a father for the first twenty-eight years of my life. When I was growing up in the trailer park, my favorite anime was *Dragon Ball Z*. I would go over to my friend's house on Saturday mornings to watch it on Cartoon Network because my mother and I didn't have cable.

Quick overview: DBZ is a show about a warrior race of "Saiyans" (humans with the power of gods) who fight for universal peace against evil godly powered villains. It's awesome. Power-ups, energy blasts, fighting, screaming . . . It's every boy's dream. (And man's . . . because I still watch it.)

I gravitated very heavily toward one of the main characters, Vegeta. He is my absolute favorite. However, he is depicted in the show as extremely arrogant, full of pride, and a hothead. He is always yelling or angry, pushing himself into battles, and putting everyone down with sarcasm. At the time I had no idea, but I was imprinting this male anime character as a father figure and role model in my life. He was teaching me about what it meant to be a man.

He was big, jacked, and took no shit from anyone; people were afraid of him, but he still fought for everyone's survival. As the programming ingrained itself deeper and deeper into my subconscious, I started embodying the behavior of this anime character. Kind of crazy the level to which the human brain is programmable. I would be overly aggressive and forceful with my words. I would say condescending things to people around me. I would make sure people stayed afraid of me so that I felt safe and manly. I thought that the role of the masculine meant being aggressive, alpha, and powerful to the point of striking fear in others.

It took me two decades to finally learn that the true role of the masculine is to be kind and generous, soft but stern. To be powerful to the point of providing peace and safety for others. The true measure of a man is within the safety he is able to provide to those around him. It is in his heart to love and protect. Masculinity is not flashy cars, fighting, or sleeping with as many women as possible. Masculinity is devotion to making the world a better place. It is building a life of integrity and following a moral compass. It is creating a safe space for others to be themselves. It is in seeing people for who they actually are and holding them there. It is creating a structure in which others can choose to follow your leadership instead of forcing them to. That is the true embodiment of the alpha: caring for others.

I lacked that masculine presence my entire upbringing. I had to make many, many mistakes in relationships, in friendships, and even in broken promises to myself in order to learn and reprogram. My heart was so closed off from love because all I knew was anger and pain. All I knew was resentment for feeling abandoned by both the feminine and the masculine. I felt abandoned by both of my parents in different ways. I never felt safe to be me. I never felt safe to express how I was actually feeling.

The problem with this is that when we don't get everything out, it just builds up. So, I would get to the point where I felt I was going to explode, and I would dump the surface-level parts onto my friends and then retreat. This pattern appears in most people through saying the same thing to your friends over and over and over again because it's all you feel safe to let out. You can see how this causes a lot of friendships to end over the years; eventually people get sick of your shit when you aren't willing to put the work in to change. Then, of course, when a friend leaves, you take it personally. It reinforces the story that there's something wrong with you. You convince yourself that "they didn't accept me for who I am," knowing deep down you never showed them the real you, only your wounds.

If I'm being honest, this is still my biggest struggle: opening up and softening to express myself fully to the people in my life. It is a very deep program. I am slowly unraveling the falsehood that I am not allowed to feel certain things as a man. I'm supposed to keep it inside and be strong since I am in a leadership position. Men don't have the right to be human.

One of my favorite rappers, Jax, has a quote in one of his songs about being a man that says, "Unconditional love is for women, children, and dogs." What he is illustrating here is the heavy burden men place on themselves in today's world to be strong. We have it backwards. Being strong is about being open and vulnerable. It takes courage to sit in your emotions and express them without a filter. Just like it takes courage to love.

Having an absence of masculine love and a large gap in feminine love my whole life made me fear love. It made me not trust it. How could I? All it ever did was hurt me. I needed to be strong. I needed to be like Vegeta from *Dragon Ball Z* and get stronger. Fight more, build more muscle, and have more people fear me and never challenge me. Surely that would get a woman to love me and see my value. Surely that would make everyone praise and respect me. It was quite the opposite.

I was stiff, uptight, and rigid. I didn't know what it meant to relax or feel safe. Keeping my guard up was the only way I knew how to survive. Until I finally realized that while I wasn't keeping any pain away, I was keeping away love altogether. So, my life was isolated. Even in a group of friends at a party, I felt so alone. Always the one wandering from each group, walking from one circle of friends to the next circle. Feeling that my time of welcome in each group had come to its end. I just never knew myself enough to feel at home with myself. So, I never felt at home with anyone else. A wayfaring stranger walking through life with no real home base.

I had to reprogram myself to understand that it was actually *okay* to be loved. It was okay to be held and to be seen at your darkest. My friend group now makes me tear up just thinking about how loved and accepted they make me feel. Actively pushing to know me deeper so they can care for me better. Finally knowing my heart and understanding how powerful the love I have to give really is. I had to surrender back to love, let it flow through me, crack me wide open, and let myself be seen again. I had to take off my armor and remind myself that there isn't a war to be fought, only love to be felt.

A few things have really helped: Constant reminders to myself that I'm okay and safe for years. Self-soothing and sitting in my emotions instead of running from them. No longer chasing things to come into my life. Staying in my life but surrendering all of me up to the abundant flow of love in the universe. Making my way back home to my own masculine and my own feminine. Teaching myself what it means to truly embody both. Letting my own feminine love me and be loved by me. Letting my own masculine lead me and be led by me. It's all brought me to this version of myself now.

Accepting harsh truths about myself led to a real awakening—an awakening that is ongoing and that continues to change my life for the better every day.

It's August 30, 2023, as I write this page. My thirtieth birthday is November 14. I made a promise to myself that I will have finished writing this book by then. I am spending my birthday doing what I love: serving my people. This last year in my twenties has felt like its own decade in the best way. I've been the most present I have ever been in my life. It's amazing how much longer life can last when you keep yourself in the present moment. Life elongates when you stand firm in the now. Life passes us too fast when we dwell on the past and continuously worry about the future, leaving no energy to live our life as it is in front of us. My intention is to have "brought to life" every project I am currently bringing to the world before I enter my 30s. I want to go into this new era free of thought, projects, and anything else I still feel I need to bring into the world. I want to walk into this next chapter and integrate everything from the last decade of my life so that when I emerge, I come out as someone different. I've awakened to myself this last year, and inaugurating my thirties in pitch blackness and deafening silence seems like the perfect way to deepen that bond to myself. It will be another necessary act of surrender in this long show we call life.

AWAKENING TASK

Awakening is my favorite stage to work through with someone. It is by far the most challenging because everything you once thought you knew or thought you cared about dissolves. Your life can change in a split second. Who you are as a person can completely transform in the blink of an eye if you open your eyes after that blink as an awakened version of yourself. It's like walking around the house not paying attention to anything until you stub your toe on the coffee table. Instantly, you are surging with energy, completely in the moment. Fortunately for you, I've found a few ways to help with the awakening process that don't involve kicking a coffee table with your toe. The awakening process is still painful, just in more beautiful ways.

Awakening to a new version of you means shifting your entire identity away from who you used to be. Before diving into these exercises, let's talk about human behavior.

All human behavior is governed by identity. Who we believe ourselves to be in any given moment will echo in everything we do. This is a pivotal exercise I use with my students to help them fully understand who it is they seek to serve and what they desire to transform those people into. The first step is expanding what I call your "empathetic range": your ability to put yourself in another person's shoes without any constriction from your current worldviews or beliefs. We have to learn to speak the client's language from where they are instead of speaking our own language from where we are. For the sake of this exercise, we are going to figure out the three core identities you currently have for yourself. If you were a student of mine, we would psychoanalyze their ideal client based on their main struggle and reverse engineer from there.

Say the ideal client is a middle-aged family man who is more than fifty pounds overweight. We have to understand how he currently views himself, maybe even better than he does. What would he think to himself on a daily basis?

We are going to say his three core identities are as follows: a failure, someone who isn't taken seriously, and an unattractive guy.

What I want you to do is write your three core identities at the top of three individual pieces of paper. Each of these identities will come with its own set of behavioral patterns that result in the reinforcement of that core identity. Write those down too. For example, our family man who identifies as a failure might constantly take on new and challenging tasks just to inevitably overwhelm himself so that the second it gets difficult, he can throw in the towel and walk away, thus confirming to himself that he is a failure.

If he thinks he isn't taken seriously by anyone, he might have a pattern of passively asserting his ideas into the group at work, only to be shut down due to lack of confidence and proper articulation. Ultimately, this leads to "not being taken seriously"—because it was never presented seriously in the first place.

All human behavior is governed by our need to secure the identity we have created for ourselves. Nobody can reinforce a negative identity like the person who created it in the first place.

It might take you some time to identify your three core

identities and the patterns that go along with them. That's okay. It is imperative that you give this section the time and energy necessary to gain full awareness. Once you have them, take these three core identities and find out what your "helmet identity" is.

HELMET IDENTITY

There is a monumental difference between men training for battle and Spartans marching to war, between NFL players practicing at home and walking onto the field of a professional game, between Clark Kent and Superman, Peter Parker and Spiderman, and Steve Rogers and Captain America.

It's the helmet. The mask. The cape. It's the identity that shifts its wearer into someone completely different. When the helmet goes on, every remnant of the old self shatters into nothingness. They have become someone entirely new. Someone endlessly more powerful. The helmet did not give them any additional powers—it gave them permission to be powerful. To be who they were born to be.

We all have two helmets we wear: the helmet that governs the undesired self and the helmet that governs who we actually are.

The helmet identity of our family man could be "unworthy of love." Since he has identified as "unworthy of love," he has created a false identity as a failure, someone who isn't taken seriously, someone unattractive. As long as he continues to play the game with his current helmet on, it does not matter what pattern he tries to replace, because the new, desired pattern is still governed by an undesired identity.

This is why so many people fall off the fitness wagon. When the only identity you have is that of someone who is unattractive and unworthy, as soon as you start making progress in the gym, losing weight, and feeling good about yourself, you start to drift further and further away from the only identity that you know. Without an identity, we have nothing to live for, because we have nothing to live *as*. When you only know yourself as the undesired identity, once you start to drift away from it, you will "self-sabotage" to get yourself back.

"Why do I keep self-sabotaging?" I don't believe we are actually self-sabotaging. I believe we never set ourselves up to be successful in the first place. You already wrote your destiny of failure because it's who you know yourself to be.

In the problem lies the solution. Once you have your three core identities written down with all their attendant patterns, it is time for you to create your desired helmet identity.

Say our family man comes across my Instagram page and sees that I create "conscious leaders."" This piques his interest, and he starts to explore my content. He watches as I list the standards of excellence I hold for the people I work with, how everyone in my company is put on a fitness program to get in shape, and how we take ownership of the parts of the world we seek to change for the better. The man in our example has one simple internal conversation with himself, and in one simple phrase he plants a seed in his mind that will change the trajectory of his life forever: "I want to become a conscious leader."

In the moment of that decision, the desired helmet has been created. Now that he knows a conscious leader is someone who takes control of their life, holds their ground, stands up for what is right, and leads those around them to be better versions of themselves, our family man starts to take on new patterns that are governed by his new helmet.

When we revisit the "unworthy" person going to the gym, he is no longer going to the gym as an unworthy person—he is going to the gym because that is what conscious leaders do.

I read the book *Limitless* by Jim Kwik a few years ago. Kwik mentions a concept that has always rung true for me ever since: if something is true when said forward, then it must be true backward as well. That is how he learns information.

So, if a new identity can create new patterns, then new patterns must be able to create a new identity.

Once you have written down your "desired helmet," work your list from top to bottom. What are the three core identities that you have when you wear the "desired helmet"? Are you generous, lucky, or someone good things always happen to? Maybe you are now someone everyone respects, someone who always speaks their mind and has valuable insight, because that's what people who wear this helmet do.

People like me do things like this.

From there, create new sets of patterns that are governed by each identity. What do you have to start doing to reinforce the new identity in yourself? Write them out as specifically as possible. If you are having a hard time, reread your old set of patterns and ask yourself, "What would the desired version of me do?" or "How would the desired version of me feel?"

Once you complete this, you have completely mapped out the path from your current or undesired reality into your new or desired reality. Remember, identity governs all human behavior. Who we are echoes in every single thing we do. If you are experiencing undesired echoes (constant financial hardship, being taken advantage of, bad luck), it is time to take full ownership and change your identity so that you can change your reality. This is the cornerstone of awakening. Letting go of everything you are not in order to become everything you were meant to be.

CHAPTER 5

APPLICATION

Lightning round. Application is only useful once we have passed through Asleep, Awareness, Acceptance, and Awakening. As you know by now, we all (hand up!) have issues to recognize, accept, and work on before we're ready to start making power moves. But now it's power move time. This chapter is going to offer you some rapid-fire exercises and suggestions for taking the next steps to full surrender. It's a segue into the final two A's—which, I won't lie, are a lot more intense.

But first, a quick aside.

The theory of us being in a simulation gets more fun every time I hear somebody new explain it. My stance is, if this is all some sort of game, then there must be cheat codes. Right? That's what this chapter is about.

If you sit around pouting, wondering why you can't ever seem to win . . . I invite you to cheat, my friend. Yes, as invigorating and "wrong" as that may feel when you first read it. I want you to cheat. In fact, what if cheating was not only allowed but absolutely necessary in order for you to advance to the next level? What if the coders of this "simulation" we are in left us little superpowered Mario mushrooms to enhance our powers and put us back in control of our circumstances?

I can't speak for you, but that idea makes me feel giddy. Let's pop a power-up.

HARDER VS. WORSE

We are wizards of wordplay. We know just how to think and speak things to ensure they upset us the most. One of my particular favorite exercises that I work with my clients on is called Harder vs. Worse. We tend to blend these two words together, giving them almost identical meaning. They could not be more disparate opposites, and I will tell you why.

When we say, "Things have to be worse before they get better," or "I know it's going to get worse," what exactly are we doing? We are giving up the thought that we have any power over a situation. We are immediately positioning ourselves in the victim chair. If we deem something to be outside of our control, then we no longer try to correct it. There's no point in trying to push onward, because there is nothing we can do but suffer until the "thing" finally decides to pass. We take ourselves out of the arena and back into the stands, watching as a helpless spectator while life chooses what's next for us.

I always thought things had to get worse before they got better, or the famous "bad things happen in threes." But do they? Is that really a universal law? It can't be. I think our perception is off. Where things only get worse, we never try to show up at our best. Which means we will never grow. You cannot build character in the absence of effort. "Things getting worse" allows you to throw in the towel and pout like a child that isn't getting their way. "Worse" is the word we use when we choose to take life lying down and no longer stand up for what we want or who we want to become.

That's why I reframe it with my clients as things getting "harder."

When you understand that something is going to get harder, what do you do? You prepare. You practice, you train, you focus. A kid playing basketball knows that middle school basketball is harder and more competitive. When we know something is going to be more competitive, we know that we need to become more competitive to match it. When we look at a situation that is unfavorable and challenging for us, we have two choices: throw our hands up and throw in the towel until the storm passes or put our hands down and hold our ground. You cannot build strength in the absence of struggle.

Something getting harder becomes an invitation to evolve and strengthen who you are. When you're at the gym and you put extra weight on the bar, you don't think the next set is a worse set. You know it's a harder set, and you mentally prepare yourself to push through because you know on the other side is a victory. You become stronger, you have more confidence, you have more drive, and now you have increased your capacity for the load you can bear. I love watching videos of big bodybuilders when they are in front of a barbell loaded with weight that would crush a normal human being (me). What they do before they attempt the squat would be seen as questionable by most. They yell, they scream, they have their friend smack them on the back—it's full-blown anarchy. But through that preparation, they become someone else. They put on a new helmet. They call out more strength because they know that is what's needed to conquer the harder challenge in front of them.

Life isn't meant to be easy; it's meant to be beautiful. Simply put, life will get harder, but it can never get worse unless you choose for it to. We are here to build our perspective, increase our capacity for pain, and stretch our willingness to push through discomfort. If life were easy, there would be nothing worth celebrating. Don't just embrace the hard; seek out the hard. Find the next challenge that causes you to dig your heels into the ground and push just a little bit more. On the other side of every challenge will be a new version of you that stands stronger than the one that came before.

When we reach this level of strength through adversity, the beautiful growth that comes with it is always the ability to *choose* compassion and gentleness. It is the gentle giant who is most powerful. The version of you that understands the strength you have built and still chooses to be kind. The ability to choose softness is only given to those who have chosen the path of strength. If you have no strength, softness is not a choice; it is a default.

When you welcome life's hardships as a next level in your own evolution, the harder it gets, the more fun you have. The more you can start to understand that if it is "this hard" right now, it can only lead you to a place where you are the strongest you have ever been. And that, my friend, is how life can never get worse. It can only get better. You just have to give it time.

GIVE CREDIT WHERE CREDIT IS DUE

I had an interesting realization come to me from a comment I received on one of my social media posts. I had posted a reel talking about growing up without a father and the impact it made on my views of masculinity. Someone from my childhood commented, remembering me being a great friend during that time. They said my mom had raised me to be the "king" I am today.

While that was great to read and hear for multiple reasons,

something stuck out to me and didn't sit right. I love my mother; she did everything she could to give me a great life, but she did not raise me to be a king. She raised me until the age of about sixteen, and I was the furthest thing from a king then. Quite the opposite, as I'm sure you've gotten by reading this far into the book. I had to put an enormous amount of work into building myself up to the man I am proud to be today.

At what point do we stop giving the credit for who we are to our parents and start giving it to ourselves? For me to accept that my mother raised me to be the man I am today would be to disregard all of the painful lessons and work it took to transform into him. There comes a point where how we were raised can no longer be leveraged as an explanation for who we are. We must get to the point of extreme ownership for why we are the way we are, whether good or bad. That is not to bypass the fact that trauma or programming can be present without our awareness. It is to say that we are fully in control of how we choose to show up in the world. We have to give credit where credit is due and nothing past that.

If we continue to give all the credit to our parents because they "raised us right," we start to downplay everything that has made our newfound evolution satisfying. If all our growth and character development is credited to our parents, what the heck are we doing anything else for? Our parents raised us to understand the world in the way that they understood the world. For some of us, that was a head start. For others . . . well, maybe not so much. Regardless of how we started, how we navigate the world now is in our own power. If we choose to say, "I am this way because I get it from my parents," that isn't on your parents—that's on you. It's you choosing to seek sympathy instead of success. You're giving too much credit where credit is no longer due.

This concept has two sides, of course. After a certain age, we start giving too much of our conscious evolutionary credit to our parents, but we do the same with our lack of evolution. You have to start giving yourself all the credit for everything you do, every way you think, and everything that is currently in your life right now. We deserve to finally give ourselves the full credit for all of it. We can be extremely grateful and appreciative of what our parents did for us, but now it's time to be grateful and appreciative for everything we have done for ourselves. Doesn't that feel good? It might not if your life isn't in great shape, but the ability to give yourself full credit for the fact that your life isn't the way you want it to be is the exact thing that gives you the credit to be able to change it.

Giving credit where credit is no longer due is giving your power to something that has no need for it. It is a wasted use of our most precious resource: your energy. By taking full ownership of all the bad you may currently be experiencing, you bring your power back to the situation. By taking full ownership of all the good you may currently be experiencing, you are putting more energy and power into your ability to create more of it.

I don't know about you, but I spent a long time giving other people credit for everything in my life. Once I started giving myself all the credit, whether it was good or bad, the bad eventually turned into good, and the good started turning into great.

I cannot sit here and pretend that I could be anywhere near the version I am today without the support of all the amazing people in my life. My friends, my mentors, and my family have been there for me through some of the hardest times in my life, always offering support, guidance, and advice to help me keep pushing forward. No man is strong enough to take on the brute force of the world on his own. We need community, we need others, and we need to be needed as well. It is who we are. I can give myself so much credit, but I cannot give it without acknowledging everyone who has stood by my side as I've evolved.

I credit and honor all of you who have played a role in my life, helped me through the hard times, celebrated with me through the good times, and supported me during every building phase. Until we give the same honor and credit to ourselves for the work we have done to evolve, we will always give credit where credit is no longer due.

BEING BLESSED IS A PRAISE; FEELING BLESSED IS A CHOICE

The way you feel about your life and the things that you experience will undoubtedly cause more of those feelings to find their way to you.

I am aligned with the law of attraction, but something that really caught my attention was when I stumbled upon the concept of "vibrational giving" in a book I read. The act of vibrational giving is derived from a way of giving created by Buddha, I believe. The principle is that the emotion you bring to giving a gift or performing an act of service for somebody will be returned back to you.

When providing somebody a resource for their business, do so because you genuinely want them to feel the emotion of you wanting them to be successful. Do that enough times, and you will find people seeking to provide you resources because they want the same.

As I look back on the short life I have lived on this earth, I can see this played out verbatim in every situation I have ever been in.

How astounding of a realization to know that how we choose to help people automatically flows its way back to us as a byproduct.

I have never come up short when I was going above and beyond to provide value for others. However, I have always come up short when I was doing the bare minimum or doing something only to get praise or an "I owe you." (See the weeds and Skittles example in the Introduction.)

When we pair vibrational giving with the law of attraction, the unfathomable power we all possess to create any life we want becomes irrefutable. Your mind is the most powerful force on this planet, and you prove it to yourself every day. Most of us are just unaware of it. What you choose to focus on, speak about, or even wish upon others has no choice but to manifest itself into your own reality.

The brain does not know the difference between imagination and reality. So, the more you talk about your back pain, the more of it you will have. The more you talk about how much you are struggling, the more you will continue to struggle. The more you wish ill upon others, the more ill you will bring onto yourself. This power is not one-sided; it is just being channeled into one side by the majority of people. The world is inevitably becoming more and more negative, people are making themselves more miserable by the day, and as such, they want other people to be just as miserable as they are. This will only and can only bring these people even more misery. It is a cycle of misdirected power that they are incredibly in tune with—yet completely unaware of.

We want to believe it is an outside force's fault. We think it's easier for us to not have the power to create a life we want because then we can get a secondary gain from our problems.

As you will recall, secondary gain is a term used in NLP to

describe a subconscious benefit that an individual gets from staying within their problem and not fixing it. Maybe our relationship is draining us, but our gain is that we aren't lonely. Maybe you hate your job and complain about it every day, but it gets you pity and attention from others. Maybe you are struggling financially, but you have an excuse to not take a chance on yourself because you "can't afford it."

By staying ignorant to your secondary gain, you move further from your primary objective. Which, if you are anything like me, is to live an extraordinary life. Choose the blessing. Give the blessing. Receive the return.

IMPOSTER SYNDROME

Something that I have learned working with over a hundred entrepreneurs is that pretty much everybody starts off struggling with the same thing. We fall into the imposter syndrome paradox and convince ourselves that we are not qualified to do what it is we have been called to do.

I want to ask you a question: If you are being called to something, who is calling you?

God? The universe?

There is a quote that circulates around churches and speeches I have heard: "God does not call the qualified; he qualifies the called." The fact that you are being called in the first place is exactly what qualifies you for the position.

In this new age of cancel culture, the second you talk about something controversial, they demand to see your qualifications to talk about it. I see this everywhere, even on my own social media accounts. I have helped support countless individuals in overcoming anxiety, destroying self-limiting beliefs, beating imposter syndrome, scaling their business, processing traumas, building the physique of their dreams, fixing blood work, creating offers, and the list goes on and on. If I touch on a single topic here publicly, the frenzy starts.

"How dare you speak about anxiety!"

"It is disgusting for you to talk about anything that has to do with a woman's health!!!"

"What qualifications do you have to talk about business?"

The vast majority of our society believes that you are only qualified if you have a piece of paper that allows you to talk about something in particular. I believe that that is a belief. My rebuttal question to this is: Who certified the first person that started certifying everyone else?

The answer is nobody. It is a made-up concept. One person became obsessed with a topic, studied it for years, produced unquestionable results consistently, and people wanted to learn it from them directly. Did the person who invented college go to college to invent college?

I will wait.

I listened to a podcast on content creation from Alex Hormozi where he spoke about positioning yourself as an expert on your own experiences instead of an expert in general. He basically went on to discuss how speaking about our own results and processes is untouchable, but telling other people what they *should* do is where the issues lie. By saying, "This is what I've done that has worked for me, and it may or may not work for you," we become untouchable.

That is basically the entire principle behind this book and everything else that I've done in my life so far.

It can be incredibly easy to retreat from speaking about topics you are passionate about when the haters come in to tell you that you are unqualified. The real truth is that if you do not have at least one to five people that hate you for every one to 200 people that support you, you just are not putting yourself out there enough. None of this is to say that I am against people getting proper certifications, credentials, and trainings that are necessary to safely and effectively serve the people they seek to serve. The day you decide to be an entrepreneur of any kind is the day you commit to being a lifelong student. You should always be striving to learn more, study under people, join masterminds, take courses, etc. The day you stop learning is the day you stop leading.

Our imposter syndrome stems from the thought that we still have so much to learn, and we need to know as much as possible *before* we start helping others. If this is the space we operate from, we will never start serving people because there will always be more to learn. It is impossible for you to possess all the knowledge in the world on a specific topic.

Here's a secret that every high school teacher knows: You do not need a certification or a degree to help people. You just need to be one to two steps ahead of where they currently are. This is a mind-blowing lesson that I discovered from Frank Abagnale. If you do not know who he is, the movie *Catch Me If You Can* was based on his life story.

Frank was the con man of all con men. At age seventeen he left home and started forging checks, posing as an airline pilot to fly for free, faking a medical degree to get a job at a hospital, and it didn't stop there. He studied for the bar exam for two weeks and became a lawyer legally. Did he go to school and get a degree? No, he became obsessed for an impressively short amount of time and passed a test other people study years for after two weeks of work.

If you ask me, I will pick Frank as my lawyer every time due to those metrics alone.

The most notable part of the story to me was that he "evidently taught an advanced sociology class at a college for an entire month without anybody knowing the difference between him and an actual, degree-holding professor. When he was finally captured by the FBI, they asked him how he was able to teach a college class for an entire month without anybody noticing. He responded by saying it was actually very simple: he just had to stay one chapter ahead of the students. He was just one step ahead of these students, teaching them what he had just learned, and they were all still learning at a capacity that did not make them question a thing.

Now I am not saying to go and position yourself as a doctor or a therapist—there are clearly fields that require schooling in order to be performed responsibly. But I think Frank Abagnale is one of the most fascinating brains in the world. He was so good at being a criminal that the FBI hired him because he was such a valuable asset.

Frank is the exact opposite of the imposter syndrome we experience in our lives.

If you have been called to serve others on a specific topic and you decide to sign that contract with God, you dedicate yourself to a life of learning.

If you have been called to open a business, that means you are the one for the job.

If you have been called, you have been qualified.

Am I qualified to write a book on my own life and perspectives on things? Absofuckinlutely I am.

WELCOME PEOPLE WHO WANT YOU TO FAIL

You will have them no matter what you do, how quietly you play, or how much you try to broaden your message so that everybody agrees with it. The issue I had when I did this was that I wasn't reaching the people I was supposed to be helping. I was so concerned about staying politically correct and not offending anybody that I put myself into a box, and my message was no longer mine.

It took me quite some time to build thick skin against the haters, but once I realized that it literally did not matter what I said and that the people who wanted to hate me would still hate me, my imposter syndrome vanished overnight. Why was I letting these people decide how I served the people I was meant to serve?

If you have a message or a calling that you feel is needed in this world, then it is your obligation to make yourself seen. In this age, social media has become the power tool for marketing. In order to market yourself properly, you have to present yourself properly. When you withdraw from your true self and your message, the people who need you can't find you.

If you are stuck in a spiral of imposter syndrome, you will always see yourself as less than. If you see yourself as a 4, you will only give a 4's effort. When you only give a 4's effort, you will only get a 4's result. When you produce a 4's result, people will start to see you as a 4. When people see you as a 4, they will treat you like a 4. And when people treat you like a 4, you will continue to see yourself as a 4. The cycle will never break until you choose to see yourself differently. It will always start with us and how we *choose* to present ourselves. With visibility comes criticism. Putting yourself out there brings judgment, hate, and controversy. But it also brings greatness, purpose, and fulfillment. Imposter syndrome is always your biggest struggle when you're making everything about yourself. When you are too hyperfocused on how you look and what people say about you. Once you get over yourself and flip your attention toward the people you seek to serve, all the other noise fades away in the background. Your life is meant to create for others, not defend from others. My job is not to defend; my job is to create.

THE SLAVERY OF ECHO CHAMBERS

I've learned a lot about myself on this journey of entrepreneurship, and I can say that developing thick skin has been one of the harder things to do. When I first began my journey, I was plagued with the need for everyone to agree with my stance on any topic I spoke about. When others met me with an opposing viewpoint, it would register as a threat to my identity—and my nervous system would shift into overdrive. I would lash back and do everything in my power to make another human being feel stupid because I could not absorb their belief. How closed-minded and shitty of me. I am sure I've hurt a lot of people in my pursuit of being "right."

It took a lot of years of constantly being ridiculed by trolls and living with a panicked subconscious need to prove them wrong every day before I finally started to find some clarity. I talk a lot with my students about awareness and self-mastery, as I have found these to be some of the basic fundamental principles for creating wealth in your life. The trolls are always going to be there, and for some reason we seem to give them our power. Interestingly enough, I am fortunate enough to be able to acknowledge that I used to be one—so I know just how weak they actually are. This has created a lot of space in my responses and a lot of empathy, knowing the sad state they are operating in.

Going about your business and viewpoints in the hopes of receiving echoes back for how incredible you are or how smart your views are is a one-way ticket to misery, self-doubt, and a chronic heightening of your flight-or-fight response. Echo chambers can become a prison and trap you in a non-expansive way of thinking. By staying open and training your nervous system that an opposing belief or conflicting view can be an opportunity for growth, you automatically expand your experience. Learning that two opposing truths can both exist at the same time and both be true is paramount for the surrender process. To some people, I'm the worst. To others, I'm the best. They're both right because they both have their own personal perceptions of their truth. Sitting in what your truth is, even when it isn't the same truth for others, is what surrender is all about. I know what is true to me, and I know that it does not need to be true to you to have validity in my life. Break out of the need for an external echo chamber and open yourself up to as many opposing perspectives as possible. When I choose a stance on something, I will typically find the opposing stance and try to prove both sides right by disproving the other. What this usually does is allow me to find a more "well-rounded" perspective of the truth. The truth usually lies somewhere in the middle of two opposing extremes.

RADICAL FUCKING HONESTY

What about the truth makes you afraid of being honest?

This question pierced me when it came up in the midst of a meditation. Why do we fear being honest so intensely? I'm not talking about being "woke" and "speaking our truth" as a means to look bold and brave. I mean our real truth. The deepest depths of our souls. Standing in the face of judgment, disrespect, and pain while still holding yourself grounded in exactly what you feel.

I spent a very large part of my life trying to always think five steps ahead of what I was going to say based on what I wanted my desired outcome to be. Maybe if I said it this exact way, then this exact thing that I want will happen. This left me with hundreds of questions, things left unsaid, and more than likely a lot of pain that I never needed to go through in the first place.

How many times have you been in conversation with someone you love, and once it's over, your mind becomes plagued with all of the things you should have said or things you wish you never said? The pain of not getting your desired outcome now becomes amplified with the pain of knowing you didn't really say everything you wanted to say. You were afraid to be honest, so you diluted your truth with the hope of manipulating the situation in your favor. That is not honesty. That is acting. That is putting on a show so the crowd will believe in the character you are trying to play.

Look, I get it. It is incredibly uncomfortable to say exactly what you feel and exactly what you want, especially when you do not know how it will be received or reciprocated. We do not want to look stupid. We do not want to experience pain. We do not want to beg someone to stay.

Well, what if you were just honest?

I have a very intuitive gut feeling that the truth, for whatever reason, is the right path for all of us. (Call me crazy.) The amazing thing about being radically honest is that radical honesty has the power to open every door, lift every rug, and wash out every shadow with its bright light. The truth can be so powerful that nothing could possibly hide, even if we wanted it to. When we withhold ourselves from speaking our truth, we turn off the path that we are supposed to be walking. We can convince ourselves all day that "I am exactly where I'm supposed to be," but that couldn't be further from the truth, just like the story you keep telling yourself.

When you do not uphold your raw, fully embodied fucking truth, you will leave your life up to chance. You will walk a path that was not meant for you. You will experience loss you might not have had to experience. You will experience pain that was not meant for you. You will be forced to live your life wishing you could go back and say something different. You will be locked in the "what if" torture chamber of your mind.

All of that washes away instantly when you own your truth. Listening to the person you love tell you that they no longer feel the same for you, yet you stay grounded in how you feel and what you want—this is fucking hard. It feels impossible. We have these defense walls that we put up as a way to "protect ourselves," so we disguise our pain with anger or numbness. We receive the news with an overly emotional reaction ("How could you do this? Look at everything I do for you.") or we shut off completely to hide from the pain ("Okay, if that's how you feel, I will respect it.").

What if you dropped the bullshit? What if you stood in the middle of the pain and pushed to keep your heart wide open? What if instead of reacting or shutting down, you leaned in and loved even harder, because that is your real truth?

"Fuck that," you say as you read this.

Hear me out.

Standing in the midst of a heartbreak and keeping your heart open to your truth is the most invigorating and empowering thing you can possibly do. In today's society, we would all rather hide parts of our truth in order to appear "strong," but in my opinion, that makes you the weakest version of yourself. You are not staying aligned with your highest self and your desires.

Instead, imagine facing that news with more unconditional love and truth than you have ever known yourself to be capable of. Imagine staring into the eyes of the one you love as they tell you things have changed and still telling them that you are in love with them. Holding true to your pain and your love simultaneously. Growing roots and grounding yourself in every emotion that comes with this storm. When we become overly reactive to somebody in our lives, we have the same power as a leaf in a hurricane.

When you ground yourself in your truth, you will eventually make your way to the eye of the storm. The beauty and stillness inside of the devastation. For us men, this is the purest form of love we can possibly unlock for the woman in our lives. Leaning into the chaos of the storm and staying grounded in your love will allow you to see into her heart. Where you will have no choice but to be paralyzed by her overwhelming beauty.

Your roots are your truth. Your roots keep you in place. Your roots keep your heart open and still as your mind races like the hurricane.

Staying grounded in your truth does not shield you from experiencing pain in your life. It simply allows you to rest assured that whatever pain you are experiencing was meant for you without question. I choose to live a radically honest life, and I will never look back. It is the hardest and most uncomfortable way of living. Most will look at this truth as a weakness, but I see it as the ultimate strength. I can rest assured in leaving any painful conversation or interaction that I did everything in my power to get the best outcome for my highest self and everyone involved.

Because I was radically honest.

When you are radically honest regardless of the situation or what the outcome will be, what is meant to happen has no choice but to happen. You have given the universe no choice but to shift aggressively into the path of the real truth.

I am obsessed with the truth now. What I love most about the truth is that it is there whether we choose to accept it or not. At our deepest core, we always know the truth. The mind will create endless stories to protect our perceived identity from the truth, but the truth does not care. We are helpless. The truth is as powerful as death, coming for all of us whether we reject it or rejoice in it. What would your life look like if you decided to lean into the power of truth instead of running from it?

We long for love because we long for truth. "The truth shall set you free" is overused and misunderstood, but (as my friend Grant showed me when I was at the end of my rope back in Chapter 1) the truth can set you free from life playing out in a way that is not meant for you. The truth will remove everything that is meant to be removed and will bring everything that is meant to be brought, regardless of how painful and confusing. The truth can live without love, but love cannot live without truth. The ultimate love is the ultimate truth, and the ultimate truth becomes the ultimate freedom. In order for us to be free, we must be grounded in our truth while staying open in our hearts. Only from this space can we release old stories and walk into our newly found selves. Our old stories will not create new ones.

Living a life of integrity to the truth has the power to move mountains and remove all worries from your mind. Pain is inevitable, but you can rest easy knowing that the only power a man can ever possess is the ability to honor his truth no matter what is happening outside of himself. When you can do that, you no longer have to worry about controlling the outcome. The outcome becomes just as pure as the truth. It becomes absolute, while we become free to love, free to hurt, free to feel.

Radical honesty has broken down so many barriers in my life. It has opened doors to levels of love and living that I never even knew were possible.

I used to fear being honest because the truth scared the hell out of me. What would people think of me? I didn't want to offend anybody or make them upset. So, I instead chose to keep making myself upset by not honoring my truth. In doing so, I experienced more pain, heartbreak, and hate than I ever needed to experience in my life. I guess tough skin isn't such a bad thing to come out of mistakes like that, but it is my hope that I can help a few of you start to remove the veil so you don't make the same mistakes I have.

You may be thinking it's too late; you may be thinking you had your chance and you blew it. I am here to tell you that you never even gave yourself a chance in the first place if you were not being completely, radically, disgustingly honest with yourself and every party involved.

You owe it to yourself to live in the truth. You owe it to the truth to honor it and accept it. The truth has only ever wanted to do one thing, and that is to guide the universe in taking you wherever you are meant to go. The universe is our greatest ally and our strongest supporter. It will always move us exactly where we are meant to go. All it asks in return is that you stay open to your truth and trust it. All it asks is that you surrender.

WHAT IF IT DOESN'T WORK OUT?

The million-dollar question. What if I do all of this, set all of these intentions, run myself into the ground, pray every single night, sacrifice a lamb every full moon, and what I want still doesn't end up happening?

I thought we were the co-creators of our reality. So why do some of us have everything we can dream of, and others do not? What is the separation between the two parties?

I will be honest with you. I wish I had the answer, but I don't. I have had many losses, more heartbreaks than anyone should have to experience in their lifetime, and what feels like more "deaths" than lives, and yet I still somehow manage to keep waking up every morning to push onward. When our strength tells us no, the path still demands yes . . . for whatever reason.

But the question stands: What would be the point of all this if we can never get what we want? Why am I scratching and clawing for a life or a love or a job that doesn't work out in the end no matter what I do? Is this some kind of weird, sadistic game we chose to play before we came here?

The more I ask these types of questions, the more I become convinced that our souls really did come down here to experience the "shit." I think of it like our souls buying a ticket to a haunted house. We know it's going to suck. We know our hearts are going to race and life is going to scare the shit out of us, but maybe once all is said and done, we come out on the other side bursting into tears of joy with every soul mate we thought we had "lost" in this lifetime.

What if the headline of the haunted house read, "Get the FULL human experience!! Find and then be ripped away from everyone you love. Lose everything multiple times. Get so fucked up you damn near try to kill yourself to make it stop!!!!!"

Don't get me wrong, this life is beautiful. I have had some of the most breathtaking and awe-inspiring moments I can't even put into words. This life continues to open more and more for you as you continue to open up more for yourself. Our goal is not to maneuver around feelings and emotions. Our goal is to expand our capacity and depth to feel.

So, again, let's circle back to the original question: What if it just doesn't work out?

Well, what if that is the objective? I know this sounds morbid, but bear with me for a few more sentences here. When everything seems lost and hopeless, can we actually shift our headspace into thinking this might just be the experience we chose for this go-around?

I know that fucking sucks, but what if? The most excitingly frustrating thing about all of this is that we have absolutely no idea if anything we say or do or think actually even matters. Thousands of times, I have prayed to God, and the opposite of what I wanted still happened. I have done everything in my power to keep someone in my life, and it still was not enough. I have also lived with the worst of intentions and been completely self-oriented, yet still seen things work out extremely favorably in my life. What the fuck?

Right now, I see most people "preaching the gospel" of the universe no matter what time I decide to open up a social media platform. Everyone is preaching, "You are right where you are supposed to be," "divine timing is never wrong." Oh, really?

If everything is divine timing, then how is anything at all divine timing? There needs to be a distinction between things for you to know the difference between them. Or are we all just perpetuating our own bullshit and seeking validation behind "divine timing" to do whatever the hell we want? If you know what divine timing is, then what is the opposite? If we never stop to ask ourselves these questions, we will fall victim to anything that is happening to us in the present moment. We will falter on our integrity to our life's purpose or our loyalties to the life we want to be building because, well . . . if it's in front of me right now, it must be for a reason, so I must act upon it for the sake of the universe's plan for me.

Is this inherently a "bad" thing to do? Well, that would depend on us knowing if anything we do really does matter in the end. Which we don't.

The divine timing scapegoat is our way of deflecting any accountability on our actions or "mistakes." If we say, "I'm just on my path," then nobody will question us. You go a step further and say, "I'm on my spiritual journey trying to find myself," and holy hell do the floodgates of no responsibility open up for us. Our spiritual journey bestows upon us the ability to run and run hard. Like a puppy being let out of its crate to play outside. Running as fast and as hard as it can with no real objective or purpose except for a newfound sense of "freedom."

This is where we can start to find ourselves in hot water. Freedom without purpose turns into self-indulgence; self-indulgence turns into uncontrollable desires; uncontrollable desires turn into vulnerability. The thing we chased for our "freedom" has now become the very thing that locks us back into a prison.

If everything works out in the end, then how do things still not work out? I think that having these "absolute" viewpoints on everything can be comforting, sure. But is that actually real? Does everything always work out in the end? If that were true, why do we commit to anything at all? Why do we set goals? Why do we push for a better life? Why do we try to live a certain way? If divine timing is putting us where we are meant to be and everything works out in the end, then I guess we can just kick our feet up and give no fucks about anything, right? I don't know about you, but something about that just doesn't seem correct to me—but hey, maybe it actually is!

You see how we can ride on this merry-go-round for ages?

We have the power to live a life filled with integrity. A life of valor and honor to ourselves and everyone around us. The power to dive into powerful loves and relationships. The power to create lives of bliss, success, and love.

So maybe it doesn't work out in the end. Maybe we do end up never getting what we want—even if we do, it never lasts forever. All we can know for sure is that we have the ability to choose how we want to show up, regardless of whether we are experiencing a high or a low. We can decide to stand in our integrity and be the person we *choose* to be regardless of anything happening outside of us.

If it ends up not working out in the end for me, I would rather be able to look back at my life knowing that I did everything in my power to fight for everything I wanted. When we can live in that lane of integrity, maybe it does end up working out in the end. Maybe the current life you are in is meant to reinforce your strength for the next life you are going to live. We really will never know, so there's no point in trying to figure it out. The only thing left to do after that is surrender.

EXERCISES

It wasn't until I started getting back to a daily embodiment and breathwork practice that I started remembering how much more grounded I was able to be once I tapped back into my primal body. For a long time in my life, I used to dance, and I was fully in my body 24/7. As time went on and bills went up, I had to move away from that to push. Now I find myself right back at the place where my body feels the best moving to the beat of music. Between dancing, meditation, and Muay Thai, I don't have nearly as much time to even try to stay in my head all day.

I cannot expect someone . . . anyone, to take my lead if I do not trust myself to take the lead in the first place. I dilute my energy when I feel uneasy about a story in my head. Which means I let the story dilute the very person I am at my core. I still have a lot to learn in this realm, but I can say the things that have helped me get out of my head and back into my body the most have been:

A daily embodiment practice.

A daily meditation/breathwork practice.

Somatic movement (dancing) to at least one song per day.

Allowing myself a safe space to scream, punch, cry, feel, etc.

Putting myself into a heightened anxious state on purpose and self-soothing myself out of it.

Speaking my desires/wants/discomforts right when they come up with NO demands of others attached to them. ("When you do this, it makes me upset because it feels like you don't Y, and that makes me want/feel/think Z.")

Not taking others' emotions as personal attacks on my manhood and learning to hold space for the storm without trying to "fix" anything.

These are the "nonnegotiables" I have put into place in my life that let me FEEL my life and my body again. The single standout variable that I have to continue to master when it comes to these situations is the art of surrender.

Surrendering to the fact that it is always and only ever will rest on my shoulders to lead my life and create a safe container for those around me. I spent a lot of painful years not speaking up for what I wanted because I thought "serving" others before I served myself was the noble way of love. It has been a hard reframe to understand that speaking my wants and providing my partner an axis to move around provides the ultimate safety and freedom in a relationship dynamic. As a chronic "anxious attachment" style, it can be very difficult for me to "create conflict" and not take it personally when it arises.

To love is to surrender.

To love is to be free.

We were all put here to do the same thing in one way or another, to love.

I deeply admire and respect you for buying this book and reading this far. Thank you. I know you are meant for more. We want to help you be more.

You might not be an entrepreneur; maybe you're just someone who wants to help another business make its impact on this world. You belong, and you deserve to live your life through impact and legacy.

We are the new wave leading the new age of business. Come find us on our socials and join our mission. We would love to have you as an addition to our culture. The world needs more conscious leaders, and that is exactly what we are here to build. If you feel called to become a leader in this world because you know deep down there is something inside of you destined for greatness, reach out to us so we can help you unlock your gifts. It's time for you to serve the world the way you were meant to.

APPLICATION TASK #1

There is a high probability that, if you are reading this, you have at least one, probably seven, hard conversations that you know need to be had, but you just aren't having them. This can turn into a big energy leak quickly. Take out a journal or a few pieces of paper.

At the top of each page, write the name of a person with whom you need to have a radically honest conversation. Maybe it's a current partner that you've been unfaithful toward. Maybe it's a friend who consistently crosses your boundaries, and now you're starting to resent them. Possibly it's a family member you need to cut out of your life for a season.

No matter the circumstance, you know deep down you aren't being radically honest. You are filtering how you truly feel because you are afraid of the outcome that comes from the truth. The truth has the power to remove people from or add people to your life instantly. It is a power beyond our comprehension.

Take this piece of paper and write out exactly what you are feeling, what has been done, said, and felt, and what your truest desire is for the situation. It is crucial not to filter yourself and hold something back. It might feel a little scary for you to finally write these things out on paper and make them tangible. This is both normal and necessary for this phase of the process. Until you can sit in your own truth, you will always make someone else's truth your own.

Stop reading and do this now.

Now that you're back, take each of those conversations and number them from one on up to the final tally, beginning with the easiest hard conversation of the bunch.

Now take each of those scenarios and, in order, write down

what the absolute worst-case scenario could be from having each conversation. Do this for all of them.

Now write out the best-case scenarios likewise.

That was the easy part.

I want you to write a "deadline" for each conversation. The timeframe for accomplishing all these conversations ideally should be within sixty days or less. I know that's challenging.

The longer we take to do something, the more we ensure it will not get done. Start with conversation 1 and work your way up your list. What you will notice is that as each conversation is had, more of your energy comes back as you begin to regulate again. By the time you get to your final conversation, you will be as ready as you possibly can be.

The truth is the only path worth traveling. You will experience loss, pain, grief, depression, anxiety . . . all of it. But on the other side of surrender is serenity. Every time.

APPLICATION TASK #2

How hard is it for you to admit you are wrong?

If we never take joy in being shown ways to challenge or evolve our views of the world, we will never grow. We came here to be expansive and stretch the very fabric of what we perceive to be reality. I've experienced reality-shattering conversations hundreds of times now. At first, I would fight hard to show the other person to be evil or stupid. It was the only way I knew how to be safe in conversations that challenged my perception of what I chose to call "reality." It wasn't until I started leaning into the triggers and challenging both sides of the conversation (while also *supporting* each side of the conversation) that the filters through which I had been viewing my world started to shift.

Think about a stance you have that you believe to be "absolute." Let's take *time* as an example.

You would write down everything you know to be the truth when it comes to time: how it works, why it's right and needed, why it must exist and could never not exist, everything. Get it all down.

Once you've written that out, write the same thing but from the perspective of the exact opposite belief. In our example, you would now write about how false time actually is. How it can never exist and will always not exist, why it doesn't work, how it isn't right or needed, etc.

Once you have these two opposing beliefs written down side by side, you are going to map them across to each other. You will try, without the bias of your current beliefs, to prove both sides right—while simultaneously trying to prove both sides wrong.

For example:

> **Point:** Time has to exist, because without time we would never know when to do something or when to meet up, etc.
>
> **Counterpoint:** Time actually does not exist in that way; that's just the perception we have chosen to create around time to govern our actions and create structure that we can understand.

Continue this conversation with yourself on one to three stances you currently have. You are starting to retrain your nervous system, subconscious, and ego to stop getting worked up when someone holds an opposing view. You start to open yourself to the infinite realm of information and potential that exists in our universe. The deadliest place for a mind to be is on one track. The goal with this exercise is to expand your capacity to challenge all the beliefs you currently have.

Looking for someone or something to challenge your views can turn into a joyous game of discovery. Echo chambers never help us expand—they only help us maintain a belief.

APPLICATION TASK #3: GIVE CREDIT WHERE CREDIT IS DUE

This exercise will be quick and painful, but effective.

You are going to write down every negative thing you are currently experiencing in your life and who you currently blame for each.

An example of this could be, "I am so stressed because I always have to drop what I'm doing to go and help my sister. I have to do this because she literally can't function without me. She won't take responsibility for her life, so now I have to, and it's draining all of my energy."

Now look, I know a lot of people read books and never do the prompts inside them. If you purchased this book, I want to call you to a higher level of integrity for your own life and purpose. Put the book down and do the prompts, especially if it feels uncomfortable to do so.

Write down these scenarios for everything you can think of. Don't worry; if you think of more later, you can do this exercise again.

Next, rewrite the complaint and put yourself to blame for the entire thing. You will position yourself as the author of everything going on in the situation.

Going back to our example:

"I am actively using my sister as an excuse to put myself into states of stress and anxiety. I am unwilling to take responsibility for creating my own life, so I convince myself that I have to do everything for her because I am unwilling to do anything for myself. I am actively setting myself and my sister up for failure by doing everything for her because that is the only way I have taught myself to feel valuable, even if it is at the expense of what I actually desire. My sister is a victim of my own manipulation, and now I am going to take responsibility and let her learn on her own, because it is time for me to do the same."

Looking at these two descriptions side by side, you can see clear as day that they are the same exact situation. One is being experienced unconsciously; the other is being experienced consciously. This is the premise of the application phase of this method. Applying these methods to your everyday life forces you to wake up and start talking, walking, and thinking differently. When we do that, we change where we place our attention. If where you place your attention is where you place your energy, then finally putting all your attention on yourself will bring all your energy back to you.

Now that you've taken responsibility and power back as the creator of your life, you have the ability to create any new experience that you choose.

Write down one way you will never let yourself think, act, or feel again. Keep that slip of paper with you.

CHAPTER 6

ASCENSION

After everything went down with the breakup I described in Chapter 1, things just seemed to keep happening. In the span of five days, I had lost my relationship, my friends, the majority of my local clients, my home, my dog . . . and someone had opened up my crypto wallet on my desktop computer and sent $248,000 worth of crypto (all of my assets) to a random untraceable wallet.

I had lost everything.

I frantically signed a lease for the first available apartment I found in San Diego, packed up a U-Haul, and drove across the country to start my next chapter. The U-Haul was old and outdated and didn't even have a working stereo, so I just drove with my AirPods in, listening to depressing breakup songs the entire trip. Thanks, Adele.

There was something oddly therapeutic about knowing that every second I kept driving, I was getting further and further away from that situation. After I got to San Diego, I felt like I was home again. I felt like I was ready to really grow as a man into this next chapter of my life and serve people better.

Then the real storm hit.

Social media posts started to pop up, one-sided lash-outs at me for my mistakes, with deflection around any mistakes from the other end. I was painted as the bad guy, the monster, and maybe I was. I just know I wasn't the only monster in the story. It was very hurtful to hear someone I loved attacking me at what seemed like every chance she could. This continued for about two months, with social media backlash, accusations, nonstop one-sided stories, etc.

It felt like I was drowning and there was no way I was ever going to be able to catch my breath. Yet, something kept telling me to remain silent and not engage. This was exceptionally hard for my ego because all I wanted to do was cast it back the other way to try and "save" my image. But I had a hard time lashing back at someone whom I had loved for the last three years, even amidst all the pain. I couldn't see the justification in ruining someone's life publicly just to try and deflect some attention away from the mistakes I had made.

It was arguably one of the harder things I've ever had to do, but something just kept telling me to remain still—almost as if entertaining the unnecessary drama would distract me from something. Something that I needed.

I kept coming back to one word over and over again: surrender.

I think people misinterpret what it means to surrender. The definition of surrender is to cease resistance to an enemy or opponent and submit to their authority. I think this definition is wrong, or at least not fully complete.

Surrender in one view can be seen as weakness or defeat, which is what most people believe. I choose to look at it in a different light.

A warrior can only charge fiercely into battle if he has fully surrendered to the fate that God has set for him. By surrendering to forces greater than himself, he frees himself up to the present moment, fighting with no fear. A warrior that has not surrendered to whatever may be fights with timidity. He cannot fight fully and cannot carry out his life to its full potential. He will always worry, which means he will always be constrained in some way.

To surrender is to understand that everything that has ever happened to you up to this point in your life, even the things you thought you would never get through, were there for a purpose far greater than you can understand. The warrior knows this. He does not dwell on what was nor worry about what is to come. He accepts the fight in front of him, when it is in front of him, with courage, knowing he can only control himself and nothing else. To surrender is to be free. To be all-powerful. To surrender is to be unaffected by that which is outside of your control. To surrender is to open yourself up to messages that you are meant to receive.

A few weeks later, I received two text messages from two separate friends. They had sent me a video link to a promo of an all-men's church retreat happening here in San Diego. Both of them included a follow-up text along the lines of, "I think this is exactly what you need."

I scoffed at the thought of showing up to an all-men's Christian church retreat to praise God. Where has God been this whole time? If God was real and loved me, then what the hell was all of this that I just went through?

But I believe in synchronicities. Having two friends—who both know I am the furthest thing from religious—independently send me texts about the same event was enough for me to say, "What the hell." I bought my ticket.

Now, up to this point, I was a believer in the "universe," not God. However, I always respected people speaking to whoever they felt they needed to speak to for guidance. I told myself that I was going to go into this retreat with a completely open heart and mind and be fully immersed in God for the weekend. If God wants me here, then I am sure He will let it be known.

So began the weekend. This Christian retreat was a very physical contact sporting event of competitions, which I thoroughly enjoyed. There were about fifty-five teams of fifty or so men all battling it out for first place. My team ended up taking second place . . . I know, we still lost. These church guys aren't so bad after all.

Each night we all met under a massive tent with a stage, monitors, speakers, etc. They had pastors and speakers come up to preach to us.

As I began to soften my wall, it was as if each pastor was speaking directly to me. In my eyes, nobody else was in that tent except me. Then the pastor said, "The Holy Spirit just came into this tent. Everybody stand up, raise your arms in the air, and invite the Holy Spirit into your heart," or something like that. You get the point.

So, I closed my eyes, put my hands up, and whispered, "God, if you are here and need to speak with me, please tell me what I need to hear. If you're real . . . I really need to know right now."

As I finished my whisper, I felt a heavy hand lay on my left bicep with enough pressure for me to open up my eyes and turn around to see who was responsible. I turned around and was stunned to see nobody standing there. Chills traveled up my spine. I distinctly remember feeling that they were traveling up instead of down because I had never experienced that sensation before. So, I asked, "Okay, God, why? Why did you just put me through all of that?"

Then I heard Him. Words spoken clear as day to me.

"Because you weren't paying attention."

He told me He had planted a seed in my head, but I was not listening to Him. I was distracted by things in my life that were not fulfilling the purpose of my highest self. He told me that it wasn't what I wanted to build; it was what He needed me to build. Then He spoke to me about prioritizing a relationship with Him. I thought this was peculiar because God spoke to me, yet He only asked for me to accept Him. Embrace Him. He did not tell me to go to church, practice a religion, or spread the gospel. He asked for me.

That was profound to me, because I had always been slightly put off by religion as a whole. But the words He spoke just seemed to make everything in my life make sense. I guess that's why he's God.

He told me what He was asking me to build and do in this life was far too big for me to do alone and that I needed to finally lean into a relationship with Him so He may walk with me to help me.

The words were so crystal clear I could have sworn to Him that He was there, and maybe He was. I asked why I was shunned from my previous life for my mistakes, why all the hate, why all the pain, the lies, etc. Up until this moment I was still left with so much hurt and confusion, but then it clicked. I was not pushed out of any situation; I was forcibly ripped out of the situation by God. He had seen enough and tried to send me messages that I kept ignoring for too long. So, He flipped my entire world upside down. It was not until I lost everything I had previously identified with, not until I was filled to the brim with guilt, shame, and disappointment, that the father I had needed came into my life with nothing but love and arms of mercy.

My view on "the higher power" has changed over time, immensely, and I think that's ok. Not only is it ok, but it should be sought. For us to change our beliefs and views on something shows growth, open-mindedness, and the ability to view things for what they are, not just what we think they are.

I believe that whatever you need the "higher power" to be for you in a certain chapter of your life is what you will find it to be. It never needs to find you because that power can never leave you. It is around you always, but like the purity of a diamond, it is crystal clear and invisible to the eye without a light shining onto it. We feel its power, we thank it, we pray to it, we curse it, but we don't ever fully surrender to it. To surrender to this power is to let it flow through us freely. To the flow of the universe, to the power of God, to the cosmic energy we all can tap into.

Energy is a flow, a law. It cannot be destroyed; it can only be transferred. Just like our belief systems. We cannot destroy a belief—we can only transfer our belief into something better or more powerful.

I think God finally came to me in the form of the Father because I was finally at a point in my life where I could get no further without having a father figure in my life to lean on and guide me. Growing up without a father was something I never felt "less" about. But that's the funny thing about life: you never truly know what has been missing until it shows up.

He came to me as a father to show me the power of a father's unconditional love and support, a father's guidance for the greater good of myself. To put my faith in somebody who knows better than I do, a figure to whom I could bow down my knee and finally surrender all parts of my life.

I had felt alone my whole life, and now I just felt . . . different.

God does not want you to prosper in *some* things. He wants you to prosper in *all* things.

God is a miracle worker for those who have surrendered to his power in every area of their lives.

Although He never once asked me to start attending church, something called me anyway. I am a proud member of Awaken Church in San Diego, run by two amazing pastors, and I am so incredibly thankful to have found them. Awaken Church truly changed my entire life.

Every Sunday it was like God was there giving me another download for what my next step was supposed to be. Breakthrough after breakthrough started occurring. Blessing after blessing kept finding me. I was in utter disbelief at this power I was tapped into.

I'll be honest though. The tithing part of church really did not resonate well with me. I thought this was just an incredibly genius business idea, and boy was I jealous. You know my story by this point. Even though I have achieved success further than I ever believed possible, I have always remained frugal with my spending. I am very particular about my finances, and I am very security-driven.

So, I had resistance. Until I had a dream.

In the mentorship work I do with clients in their businesses, I have them set SMART goals. Specific, Measurable, "As if" it's happening now, Realistic, Timed. The process is about using your reticular activating system (RAS) and your subconscious to help you achieve goals you would think were otherwise unachievable. You must know your outcome. In NLP, "knowing" is derived from seeing, hearing, and feeling something.

We discuss these goals and put the client into the state they would be in if these outcomes had been achieved on this day. I then visualize what they will see, what they will hear, conversations that will be had, and how they will feel when this outcome is achieved. This is an incredibly powerful practice for setting outcomes in your life or business.

Interestingly enough, I had a dream about finances. One of my goals for this last year was for the company to do $250,000 in a month. I thought, *This goal definitely stretches my leadership ability, but I also know I can make it happen.*

So, I had an intensely vivid dream in which I saw a number in the bank account: $248,649.15. In the dream I saw myself looking at my phone, feeling in awe of how it got there, and heard myself saying, "Holy crap, I can't believe it happened." When I woke up that morning, the number was still oddly engraved in my brain. I could recite it for days afterward.

During this time, I was selling one of the homes I had bought a few years prior in San Diego. My expected return on this property was around $125–140k net. I was stoked for this. The house finally closed, and I asked for the money to be sent to me via check. The next day I got in my complex elevator, walked out to the mailbox, and there inside was the check from my first ever property sold. It was a good day; little did I know it was about to be a great day.

I came back up to my apartment and opened the envelope, impatient to see the numbers. To my utter disbelief, the check was for $244,582.52.

"What the . . . !?" I gasped.

How in the world is this check over $100,000 more than what I was thinking I would get for the house? But I knew why. I knew exactly why.

"Thank you, God" just started flowing from my mouth, uncontrollable in my disbelief. Yet, I was still confused as to why the number I saw in my dream was different.

Five days later I received a second check in the mail from the escrow company. It was the exact difference, putting the total net cash at $248,649.15.

God had undoubtedly blessed me, and I knew why He did it. For you cannot be frugal when you are walking with God. You cannot withhold from Him. To do so is to withhold His blessing from yourself.

So, I did exactly what I needed to do, and I tithed $25,000 to the church, 10 percent. It was nerve-racking, but I also felt a massive release once I pressed the send button. As if that final part of my resistance to everything He could offer me had softened into a surrender state.

I think that when we tithe, we think that what we give we get back tenfold because "that's God's power." If we don't get exactly that, then we lose faith. From my experience, God is not here to give us what we want. He is here to provide us with what we need. Only then can we take action to build with God, to get everything that we want.

We cannot wait around for blessings, the universe, or God to come and save us. He can help, but we have to give Him something to work with. The universe does not flow through the lazy man; it passes him by. The universe responds to the warrior. To him who chooses a path of faith and honor. It took me twenty-eight years to come to this full embodiment and realization. Some of you are younger than me, some older, and some the same age, yet I am sure you all have struggled with the notion of "wasting" years in a situation, not being where you are "supposed to be."

To believe this is to disbelieve in something greater than you.

Don't get me wrong—there is a space between fate and free

will. Fate is what you were destined for; free will is what you decide to do about it. By withdrawing into the victim mentality of not being where you are supposed to be, the universe has no choice but to keep you in that exact spot until you become present and look for the lesson you are supposed to be learning. I have learned that there are levels to our evolution as human beings. The reason that people get stuck at a certain level is because they stop looking for the door that will take them to the next.

You must surrender to the principle that you are exactly where you are supposed to be, always. This is fate. Free will is how long you choose to stay there. Your fate will follow you as you begin to tap into your highest self and push upwards for the life you were born to live. You have to be fearless while walking your own path instead of worrying about what everyone else's path looks like.

It takes courage to walk your own path. If you can be talked out of it, it was not given to you by God. Learn what you need to learn so you can move on, even if it is a painful lesson. Pain has always been one of the best teachers. Let it teach you, not rule you.

It's funny how we tend to assume that if we don't have life rolling out perfectly in front of us, then we should feel misery or defeat. Your life is, and can only ever be, what is happening to you right now. Just as the warrior must focus his presence in the moment of battle, you must focus your presence into this moment of your life. This moment is your battle. You have to fight for an extraordinary life every single day.

The thing about a life like this is that you have to be willing to do what the majority of other people are not. We hear this all the time, but it bears repeating.

I am blessed beyond belief for the life that has unfolded in front of me. I am not proud of all the faces I have worn throughout my life, but I stand here proud of how I turned them into lessons to build me into the man I am today.

You are not what you have *done*; you are what you have *overcome*.

You are reading this book, and that makes you very special to me. I truly mean that. Thank you for supporting me and dedicating your time here. Most people never even finish a book after they start it.

I have never written before, so when I was called to turn my mess into a message for someone out there, it took me a long time to finally take action. I knew that somebody, even just one person, would be helped by learning from my mistakes and experiences.

I think that's the reason we make these mistakes in our lives. They were made by you to share the lesson so others can be enlightened and not go down the same path. We create shame and guilt around our mistakes and try to keep them as secrets. I believe that if we never speak about them or use those stories to teach, then all of that pain will have been for nothing. I can't accept that. All of my pain and the pain I've caused others must have a positive purpose. I don't think it erases our wrongdoings; I just think it gives a better ending to the story than if we were to just leave it where it died.

What I want for you is the best life that you could possibly have. I don't pretend to know all the answers. I'm still figuring all of this out as I go along.

What I do know is that this power that I have experienced in my life is there for you as well.

What I do know is that you are powerful beyond anything you could have ever imagined.

What I do know is that you are one decision away from letting go of everything that is holding you back. One decision away from creating the life of your dreams.

All I ask that you do is finally surrender. Surrender to whatever or whoever you speak to right now. Surrender to the notion that you are exactly where you are supposed to be, and it is not possible for you to be anywhere else.

This life is short. I think our time on this earth is so minuscule in the grand scheme of things because if we really knew how to harness the raw power of this source, our lives would seem endless. What if that's the secret? A hundred years can feel short or can last for eternity if you choose it.

I know that you were meant for more. I know that prosperity is a mandate placed upon your life by a force greater than all of us, and I hope that after you read this book, you will no longer ignore the fire inside of you that you have been afraid of letting out. I hope that you surrender to that fire and let it engulf you. An extraordinary life is supernatural because it goes above the natural laws of life as we know it.

Everything you need is already inside you. That is the power that you feel. The world needs that fire. The world needs you.

All that is left for you to do is surrender. Once you do that, the world will be yours.

Trying to swim against a rapid will ensure your death, but surrendering to its raw power and then moving with it takes you very rapidly downstream. This is also true for the universe and God's power. You need to make room for it. If your hands are full because you are holding onto other things from your past and current life, nothing new can be placed in your hands.

Letting go of something after it has served us does not mean we value it or love it any less. If you keep a hammer in your hand because it helped you put a nail into a wall, you are going to have an exceptionally hard time changing a tire. The same is true for the people in our lives.

I like to think about people in our lives as leaves on a tree. During the early ages of a tree's life, the leaves stay very close together. As time runs its course, the tree will continue to grow and expand, and some of those leaves will grow further and further apart. Those leaves will never see each other again in their lifetime. That does not mean that one leaf has to hate the other or that it must hold onto what once was. When you take a step back to look at the tree as a whole, those leaves are all still part of the same beautiful picture. That is your life. If we drew a rope around the branches to keep the leaves together, the tree would never see its beautiful growth potential realized. We must surrender to forces greater than ourselves and allow the branches and leaves to grow without resistance. Only then can the tree live out its life in full capacity.

You must choose to feel blessed for everything that has ever happened to you in your life because it is a part of a bigger picture that you cannot yet fully see. Every experience and every person has played the exact role they were meant to play in your life. If they hadn't, you would not be reading this book right now.

If we focus on being a victim of our circumstances, we will only ever be a victim. You must choose to be a warrior of circumstance and take action to always move forward. Instead of asking, "Why is this happening to me?" we must reframe the question. "What am I supposed to be learning right now?"

Pain is all I've ever known. It was the only thing I knew how to feel. It was the only thing that would prove to me that I was alive. My entire life I have felt alone. I had friends, but very few have I known on a level deeper than the surface.

I want to thank Annie for putting pressure on my inability to truly feel. She was the only person in my life that had ever seen me for me and knew there were walls up everywhere else. The only person that ever loved me enough to challenge me to that extent.

Annie and I started officially dating five days after meeting for the first time. Two days after that, we said "I love you." We didn't get caught up in whether we were taking things fast or slow. We just lived hard and fearlessly. We just got lost in the effortless dance that was always playing out between our souls.

But about two months in, I started feeling . . . different. A few minor things had happened that I chose to let "trigger" me, giving me confirmation that my walls needed to build back up.

I became distant and was unable to keep myself present. My emotional availability became non-existent as my mind would never stop thinking about possible scenarios that could be happening behind my back. I started becoming very insecure inside my own head, wondering why she was with me, what she was gaining from me, and what I was doing that was keeping her around. Surely it had to be something I was "doing" or providing for her. I could not consciously wrap my head around why I felt this way or why I was starting to do everything that I was doing. My conscious mind could only come to one main conclusion: I was triggered, and I was afraid.

I was afraid to let my walls down and truly feel. Afraid to be fully seen because to be fully seen and my true self would mean if she left, I would be hurt. So, I put this wall up to "protect me." I convinced myself every time that there was surely a logical explanation for why she was asking me to feel or telling me that she could tell I wasn't fully there with her.

My brain would give me easy stories to digest.

Maybe you're just not fully over your ex yet. It will come with time.

Maybe she wants you to be somebody you are not.

On the contrary, she was challenging me so that these walls would come down and I would just be me, the real me. She saw glimpses of that version of me a few times when I would forget to have my guard up. I think that was a big part of what made her stay for as long as she did. She had hope that I would come home to myself.

"FEEL," she would always say to me. It was the word of our relationship, yet I always had a block.

As the relationship went on, it stayed beautiful. Our relationship was short but lived with depth. It was the purest connection of soul I had ever felt with another human being. However, as time passed, the connection started to tighten, as if in a chokehold by a hand I could not see, squeezing the life out of something that was once so full of life.

We started to grow distant, and my stories of why I needed to protect myself became stronger and stronger. On one Sunday night, I lay in bed staring at the ceiling. She was next to me, asleep. I could not shake the sense of something feeling very off. My mind took me to the same places it always did.

There has to be someone else.

She's following all these jacked guys on social media. There must be something going on.

I woke her up and expressed that I felt something disconnected between us.

As we started conversing, half asleep, she gently spoke that her body felt as if it was rejecting the relationship. Annie has always been an immensely powerful and attuned person. Something I admire very greatly about her.

She said her nervous system constantly felt stressed now, and that her body was giving her a very aggressive "yes" to us no longer being together.

I was crushed but not confused. I knew exactly what she meant and why she felt the way that she did. No feminine can feel secure when the masculine is not grounded and assured in themselves. It always started with me.

We fell back asleep. When my alarm went off Monday morning, the tears started to flow. As I helped her gather up her things and walked her and the dog out to her car, we stood in each other's arms and stared at each other. Pulling her face to mine to be present for one final kiss before our goodbye. She looked back at me and placed her finger on my forehead gently.

"I hope you can get out of there one day," she said softly. "I love you."

I kissed her forehead and walked away. Wishing things could have been different but knowing that they couldn't be.

This was the first breakup I had been through that didn't end horribly. Which made it hurt the worst.

She knew that it was time for both of us to have an inward journey of ourselves. I know that walking away was not easy for her. I am so grateful that she was patient with me as long as she was.

HOW TO BE ALONE

The day Annie left, I started becoming omni-aware of my thoughts and patterns. I noticed that once I got back into my apartment, it was, "Okay, I wonder who I can text to come over tonight so I don't have to be alone." Whoa, WHAT? I stopped myself.

I started observing my initial programming very curiously.

I was sitting in the heavy feelings of pain, loneliness, abandonment, and longing for something I could not have.

Why would she leave if she loved me? I kept asking myself.

I needed to let off steam, and now I was freshly motivated to get into great shape again, something I realized I hadn't felt in a while. So, I went to the gym. While I was there, a set of bicep curls strung together one of the most profound breakthroughs of my life.

I was halfway through the set, right when it started getting challenging (this is where you start to actually progress), and a thought came into my mind: *That's plenty. Let's go ahead and put it down now.*

As I sat there mid–bicep curl, I realized that this is how I had been approaching my training for a good while, almost the whole time I had been in my relationship with Annie.

Then it all hit me like a freight train. When I met Annie, I was in great shape, business was booming, and I was the most grounded and confident I had ever felt. Yet about two months in, everything started to come up again. Insecurity, sacrificing things for myself, putting my power outside of myself . . . the list went on. I realized as I looked back on all of my other relationships that they had all ended the exact same way.

It was a pattern. Looking even deeper, it was actually a recipe.

Pain is all I have ever known how to feel. I convinced myself that I could not love fully, or she would leave and I would get hurt. Yet that story resulted in exactly what I told myself I was afraid of.

The question became, "What if that's not actually what I am afraid of?"

What if I had a deep-rooted subconscious desire to carry out a recipe that inevitably led me back to pain, loss, longing?

What if I actually loved it on a subconscious level?

My ego could not grasp it. My ego hated my willingness to accept that I actually wanted this to happen and had no idea.

I saw my pattern: Pain and loss. Longing ensues. I become motivated again. I build myself up in all areas.

I found Annie at my peak of life, and she matched that perfectly, like a puzzle piece. Then once my subconscious got to the point of understanding "this relationship is sound," it immediately started looking for ways to start pulling me back down behind these walls.

I stopped pushing myself as hard in the gym, so I watched my physique backtrack, causing me to feel a deep insecurity in my appearance, which led to projections outward on what she must be thinking about me and other men who had what I no longer did. Then I could easily take the smallest of things and blow them up in my mind (subconsciously) to justify the story of exactly why I needed to be pulled back in behind these walls—knowing at my core that this is exactly what I needed to do to eventually push her away and get back into the feelings of pain, loss, and longing that I loved so very much.

I started observing things that she didn't like and would subconsciously act out in that way. *Why the hell are you saying this?* I would say, in the back of my mind, even as my mouth spoke the words. My subconscious was actually just fulfilling a loop of desire I did not know was there. To feel pain, loss, and longing.

We consciously call it self-sabotage and get frustrated, but our subconscious is actually just acting out of unconditional self-love. I know . . . weird, right?

Let me give you an example that helped me make sense of this.

Let's say I have a son (my subconscious), and he overhears me on the phone, upset, talking about how I just want my damn car cleaned. My son (subconscious) hears my desire (even if I am not aware of it) and says, "I love Dad, so I am going to go wash his car."

Now, my son does not know to what extent I want it cleaned, and he also has no idea how to clean a car because I have never given him clear instructions. He has seen his mom clean things over by the sink before and thinks that surely that is where the tools must be. He looks under and pulls out dish soap and steel wool, then makes his way outside to the car.

As he starts to clean the car, he is filled with love for me because he just can't wait to show me that he did what I asked without me even knowing it was getting done.

Then I walk outside and see the paint of my car all over the driveway, as it has been scratched off with aggressive, full-body strokes of steel wool. My first instinct (most of ours) is anger and frustration.

"Why would you do it this way?" "This isn't what I wanted!" "Why does this keep happening to me?" "I am so irritated with myself (my son)."

With that reaction, we can assume that my son (subconscious) is now heartbroken. He bows his head and scrapes his feet back inside up to his room, thinking, *I wonder how I can try to clean the car again so that Dad (me) will finally just acknowledge what I am doing for him.*

Now let's take it to scenario number two.

I walk out onto the driveway and see my car scraped up and the paint ruined, my son (subconscious) standing there with a big smile on his face covered in soap. This time I choose to praise him for the work he has done at fulfilling my desire (that I did not properly express because I did not know he was listening so closely).

"Wow, this is amazing!!! This is exactly what I was asking for! I actually love the fact that you cleaned it this way. How about we clean it like *this* next time?"

So, what happened here?

Even though I (consciously) did not ask for my desire to be fulfilled this way, my son (subconscious) fulfilled what he thought I was truly wanting. It was all out of the deepest form of self-love.

Once I am able to accept my son (myself) fully and accept that he was fulfilling exactly what I asked him to, I can release his grip on wanting to prove his love for me that way. Even better, I can now replace the old desire with a new desire that I can consciously be aware of. By accepting my son (my whole self) fully and without judgment, shame, or guilt, I was able to remove all of the power this "cycle" possessed over my life. I was able to laugh at the fucked-up paint job and laugh at myself for getting what I asked for.

I have desired my whole life to not feel, to not love or be loved, because I consciously thought I was afraid of pain—only to realize that pain is always going to be there, whether I love or not. I was only accepting pain and withholding myself from love altogether.

I want to take this concept up a little higher.

In the Bible it says that God created us in His image. We see God as the creator and ourselves as the co-creators.

My goal with sharing this stance is not to change anybody; it is simply to articulate the breakthrough of my life.

If God made us in His image, then that would mean that His power as Creator is inside us already. So, what if we are both creator and co-creator interconnected?

Your subconscious mind is the creator. It is God's power

bestowed upon you. Just like God and His power, we know it's there. We can feel it, but we cannot consciously make sense of it.

Our subconscious creates for us without us even knowing it is there. Much like my son went to wash my car without me consciously being aware of it, our subconscious does this for everything. It puppets our conscious mind, which is why we can never understand why we "keep self-sabotaging." Imagine a puppet unaware of the puppet master.

What if I told you that your power lies dormant until you can fully accept and embody it? What if when you do, it aligns creator and co-creator so that you can create any life you want without even being consciously aware?

My creator (subconscious) had been creating a particular life based off of my desire the entire time. Until I was able to fully see that on a deep level and fully accept my son for washing my car "wrong," I was not able to change my desire. I would be destined to fulfill a desire I was unaware of my entire life—and I would never stop calling it bad luck.

If God made us in His image, then that means we have the creator power of God.

If God created the universe, then that means that our universe is our creation.

There is a theory that there are an endless number of alternate universes all happening at the same time. I fully believe this, and I believe that every one of us is in our own universe, which we have the power to create and bend at will.

We convince ourselves that our power is without us, but it is actually within us. We pray and ask God to give us strength and for the universe to give us a sign. Yet God gave us all the strength we need. We just have to accept that we have been creating our entire lives.

When you align the creator (subconscious) and co-creator (conscious) you don't ask the universe for favors. You make commands, and your universe will begin to shift around your desires. It has been doing this since the day you were born, but you are only now fully aware of it. Which means you control the canvas.

I spent my life up to this point drawing it out in fear and then coloring it with pain. Wondering why the picture always came out the exact same. I did not know I was the one holding the brush, capable of rinsing those colors off and choosing new ones.

Imagine if you replaced the mistaken desire with something you truly wanted. Imagine if I replaced my desire for pain with a desire for endless love and depth in my relationships.

All you have to do is surrender to the truth. Surrender to your power that you have known deep down was there all along. The power that has been afraid of you. That you have been rejecting because you have not fully understood it.

I want you to sit and verbally accept yourself and every desire you have been fulfilling in your life. Even if your ego fights you and it doesn't feel good. It might feel bad to say, "I actually love keeping myself poor because it keeps me on edge and anxious. I am so good at it that the second I start to get ahead, I instantly find a new bill or expense that swallows it up, so I go right back to anxiety."

Maybe you can "never lose weight," but you secretly love the victimhood and helplessness. You love the rush of emotions because that is what makes you feel alive, just as pain did for me.

By accepting, you are fully empowered. By rejecting, you are fully resistant.

This breakthrough changed my entire life. But by losing the one I loved, I gained the wisdom I needed to keep her in the first place. Annie showed me unconditional love in ways I never even knew existed. Not just for myself but for her as well. To this day she is one of the most incredible humans I have ever had the pleasure of knowing. Which is why this book is dedicated to her. She taught me real surrender, she taught me what it meant to "feel," and she taught me that everyone has a journey that eventually needs to be taken alone.

All I had to do was surrender.

THE PENDULUM SWING FROM THE MASCULINE TO THE FEMININE

A few decades ago, we were in a hyper-masculine era of our culture. Now when we look around, we see that we have swung to the other side toward the hyper-feminine.

Neither of these is helping us get anything productive done.

However, in order for the pendulum to center itself, it must go through the full motion of the swings first. So here we are in a hyper-feminine world. The kids can no longer win first place; they must all win for participating. The standards we once set for excellence are now obsolete. Being excellent is a rarity because excelling at anything is now frowned upon. When one gets praised for excelling, we now have to consider what all of the "below average" performers must be feeling.

We are removing supermodels from billboards and leaning into the "body positivity" community so that everybody feels seen and heard. We do not want excellence and beauty to stand out; we want to dilute it so everyone can feel the same.

We want to embrace the beauty of every form of self-destructive abuse, emotional sabotage, and unhealthy coping mechanisms. We want to accept all the parts of ourselves that are the hardest for us to accept because then we do not have to feel the urge to improve. If I can get everybody to agree that I am beautiful "just the way I am," then I can indulge in endless acts of self-hatred that physically manifest onto my appearance, and nobody can tell me otherwise, or they will get canceled.

Cancel me. Please.

My message is meant to be triggering. It is up to you whether you let it trigger you into evolution or trigger you into offense. I do not judge anybody for anything they do. If you are three hundred pounds overweight and have convinced yourself you love yourself and your life, who am I to stop you?

Now look, I am not going to sit here and say that it's the "feminine energies'" fault that we are in this . . . interesting state. In fact, when balanced and wielded properly, the feminine energy is arguably the most powerful force in existence. Everything around us is filled with the power of the feminine. The ocean and its ability to be calm, beautiful, terrifying, merciless, and all-powerful at the same time is the perfect concept. The feminine energy is beautifully articulated by the ocean. The more surface level you stay, the more vulnerable you become to the harsh storms and chaotic waves of her power. The deeper you dive into the feminine waters, the more stillness you will find.

We are a surface-level society. We cannot handle truth, we cannot handle facts, we cannot handle emotions, and we cannot handle discomfort. We are being led down a path of superficial stimulus that is creating an even more superficial world. Kids don't play outside anymore. If they do, it's to film a fucking dance on TikTok. Where did we go wrong?

I presume it's due to the radical sides of the coin thinking that their way of living is "all-knowing"; if anybody questions it, they are labeled as toxic. Cancel culture makes me laugh more than most things. You are telling me that because somebody has a stance in their own personal life that bothers you, we now run and "rally the troops?" We cancel somebody and ruin their life? For what purpose? Validation that we can't get from anything other than watching others burn?

I am all for personal responsibility, but the way we are shifting our thinking is back to that of children bullying the kid on the playground who's wearing the weird puffer zip vest when it's 95 degrees outside. (It's me. I'm the puffer zip vest kid.) We are living a life of fear. When we live in fear, we keep a weapon in hand at all times to wound whoever we can. We stab at anybody who comes within our reach because we do not know what it means to be at peace. We are too afraid to bring people in and empower them anymore, so we must send an army out to tear them down so we can feel better about our own lack of evolution.

Enough is enough. Nobody stands up for anything or anyone anymore. Nobody stops to question the masses and break out into their own stance. Do we not see what's happening here? They don't want people breaking away from the status quo. They are rewarding us for our mediocrity, damning us for divergent thinking, and breaking into our greatness. If you keep getting offended by someone better than you, then you have no catalyst for true growth.

Eventually something inside you has to snap. You have to get tired of being broke. Tired of your life being wasted.

We are battling between two opposite extremes, and we are all losing because of it. Hyper-femininity is just as detrimental to us as hyper-masculinity. We must find the balance between what everyone is trying to fight over. Whenever somebody is very aggressively pulled to one side on a stance, it's a pretty easy indicator that they aren't thinking of the full picture. When both sides are standing at polar opposites, the solution is more than likely somewhere in the middle where nobody wants to venture.

There needs to be sacrifice. Things need to be challenging for us. Things need to force us to move and be uncomfortable if we want to live out this experience the way we were meant to. We need to wake up and see what we are doing to ourselves.

Look, I get it. Speaking out about things that most deem "set in stone" does not make you many friends. You get attacked, bullied, and damned to hell for daring to think something different, let alone teach others your way of thinking. The truth is that I am relatively used to being hated for my stance on things and for the messages I speak. My message is meant to be triggering. My entire goal is to make people think differently and see the possibilities in a new way of living.

When we get triggered, we have only two options to choose from: we either can get triggered into offense or we can get triggered into evolution. Which one do you think our society keeps choosing?

YOUR ORACLE

Being a man in this age is brutal. There is a constant ping pong of what women want, how they value men, and how men should be showing up to maintain respect and loyalty.

Make sure you show your emotions; otherwise, you are not in touch with them—but don't show too much emotion, or else you are weak, and no woman will stay. Make sure you take control and lead—but not too much control because then you are controlling and manipulative. Take charge of your woman and ravish her—but only if she is 100 percent in the mood, and if she says no to your sexual advances, it shouldn't bother you.

Seriously, the list goes on forever. I sat there just saying "what the fuck" to myself over and over and over.

Okay, so I just need to be a dick and not care in order to get them. Then I need to start being more emotional to keep them, but then if I slip up and get too emotional, I am seen as weak, and they don't feel safe in my presence anymore.

Dare we throw money and abs into this equation? If men do not have enough money or "status," they are already off to a bad start, let alone if the guy standing next to them has a six-pack as well.

The pressure on men to be handsome, ripped, rich, in touch with their emotions while also not showing them too much, alpha but sensitive, and funny but serious can be incredibly overwhelming.

That was what I was all the time: overwhelmed. Then when I was finally myself and opened up, it would immediately result in me getting hurt. Over time I built up an armor so thick I couldn't even see myself through it anymore. I didn't care for anybody to get in. I became disconnected from my body and my primal self. I trapped myself in my head—and that is where I stayed for a long time.

As a coach for entrepreneurs, it can be all too easy to stay operating out of my head in everything that I do. My hyper-analytical mind is what I learned to use to keep me safe and keep everybody else in my life at arm's length. I recognize now how hard it was for me to even look others in the eye at that point in my life.

Intimacy scared the shit out of me. If we are being honest, that fear still lingers. I convinced myself that if I was able to analyze every move, tone, word, and action from someone, then I would be able to know what was happening before it was happening, outrun the pain, and leave. Man, what an exhausting life it has been up to this point living that way. I can tell you full-heartedly that I am still recovering from the nervous system exhaustion I put myself through with this subconscious thought that everyone was out to get me.

I was the king of reading a self-help book, trying out what I learned for a week or two, seeing amazing progress, and then disregarding it completely. Allowing myself to go right back into the same suit of armor.

The main piece I had always struggled to break through was the thought that sharing my emotions, getting mad, or speaking up when something bothered me in my relationship. I told myself that if I just ride it out and pout or show (passive-aggressively) that I am in discomfort, then my partner would change their behavior. I was trying to manipulate them to stop hurting me, but I was too much of a coward to tell them that I was hurt. What is even crazier is that I truly had no idea I was doing this because I was so in my head that my brain was firing scenarios like a supercomputer all the time. My eyes would gloss over as anyone spoke to me as my anxiety crept in and showed me 4k movies of everything that could possibly go wrong.

In my head I would constantly be telling myself: As a man, I am not allowed to feel. As a leader, I am not allowed to be weak. As a coach, I am not allowed to have my personal life burning to the ground. Yet all of these things were consistently true in my life. I thought I was the grounded, super-stable masculine by not reacting to things. All that resulted was me never being heard, never speaking my truth, and resenting myself more every single time.

I think the hardest part about differentiating a trauma response of anxiety from your own intuition is when you've always ended up being right about what you thought was happening anyway. Every time I felt something was off in a relationship, I would convince myself that, "You're just being paranoid because of the last one. This one is different. Don't bring the old into the new." And then the bomb would drop. I would find out I was right all along, and down an even deeper spiral I would go.

I became so preconditioned that once I made one misstep in a relationship, that was it. They now had their excuse to go and find somebody else, and the clock was ticking on how fast I would be able to "save" myself with a redemption so that they would stay. I lived my entire life feeling as if I was at the mercy of the first good-looking, wealthy, ripped guy to cross paths with my partner if things were not absolutely perfect in our relationship at all times. This would lead to me constantly checking in on them from a place of desperation instead of love and curiosity. I would constantly be checking social media to see if there was anybody new they were following, and I would text them certain things to see how they would respond to reinforce the stories in my head.

I felt I was easy to abandon if I made one mistake. I became so consumed by this that I stopped being myself. I started calculating my moves, my words, and my actions on what I thought would land me at the best possible outcome. This put me even deeper inside my fucking head. Emotion is energy in motion. There was no emotion behind anything I said or did. I had no energy in my head, and I was not in my body to produce motion. I was a computer. A robot.

I was so used to being denied or rejected that I would constantly seek it. Getting a no from my partner hurt, but being able to crawl my way back and get a yes again? It was invigorating. "Wow, I almost lost her, and I was able to win her back." (We are talking a four-hour time span here.) Dopamine dopamine dopamine!!

As time went on, it started to become more difficult to get back to a yes as she became disinterested in the cycles. I just kept getting shut down harder and harder. Finally, I snapped and asked what was going on. I will never forget reading via text message (yes, text message) that I was stuck in "little boy energy" and there was absolutely no desire to have sex with that, nor did it feel like energy she could trust.

Wow.

Reading that from your woman is nothing short of emasculating, but I think again that we have only two choices when we get triggered. We either choose to be triggered into offense (where most men go, as they take it personally) or choose to be triggered into evolution.

A few books I've read refer to the woman in your life as your oracle. The one who is there to show you where your shortcomings are and guide you on your path to unleash yourself. Instead of taking all of the jabs as a personal attack on my manhood, I chose to take them as intense acts of love from a woman who knows what is underneath the armor.

It shook me to my core. Not only did I know she was 100 percent right—I also knew that I knew that the whole time. I felt myself sinking back down into the same hole while clamming up into my head like I had done in the past. Not letting myself feel my emotions was actually just forcing my partner to feel them for me.

5-MEO-DMT

During the writing of this book, I had an extremely profound assignment bestowed upon my life by God. He spoke of actions, numbers, impact, everything so firmly it was overwhelming.

"Did God mess up?" I said to myself. "He must have the wrong guy. There is no way I have the capacity or the power to build what He is asking me to build."

For weeks I had back-and-forth discussions with myself, wondering if it was my own thoughts and desires just speaking their way through. Every night before I slept, every day I lived, these assignments kept flooding my mind. I decided that I needed to get closer to God on a soul level to get clarity around the things I was struggling with.

I am so incredibly blessed to have met such an amazing human who is also my shaman.

I met her at a ceremony she led to welcome the New Year in 2022. This was my first experience with medicine outside of psilocybin. During this ceremony we were administered changa, which is essentially smokable ayahuasca. I reached out to her again in hopes she would be open to facilitating an intimate ceremony with me utilizing Bufo (5-MeO-DMT). I had never ventured this far into psychedelics or medicine before, but my calling to go directly to the source for answers could not be ignored.

As I am typing this, I am on my flight back from the ceremony. It ended only a few hours ago. I wanted to get my thoughts out while I was still connected to the source.

As I sat in the ceremony room on a light-gray quilted blanket, I glanced around at all of the crystals and sound bowls she had laid out. The most beautiful music played gently over the speaker in this sacred space she had created for me. I felt so unbelievably safe knowing she was watching over me as I ventured into the unknown.

We primed with some meditation, breathing, and opening of my heart. As I let out a final breath, she held the pipe to my lips, and I began the long, slow inhale into existence. The smoke slowly filled my lungs, and my body started to tingle and feel as though it was floating into the heavens.

Most people experience a "launch" into space. I actually went through an extremely peaceful "dissolving" of the reality around me. It felt as though the veil was being lifted from my body, mind, eye, and heart. I entered into a state of pure connection with everything.

I stopped being able to feel myself swallow or breathe. Even my heartbeat became a distant memory. I witnessed both life and death happening simultaneously to me and outside of me.

After a while I was met with an overwhelming feeling of love, as if all worries or doubts or fears were blinded by the light of source. I felt pure. Full of energy and life force. I knew only love at that moment. Speaking into this white abyss, my words were answered with words, pictures, and feelings in my body.

"Are you sure you've got the right guy for this?" I spoke softly. "I don't know if I can do what I feel you are asking me to do."

I did not ask if you thought you could. I gave you the ability to do it when it was spoken.

"Okay, holy shit . . . so . . . what do I do?"

As I asked this, I felt my body completely disintegrate from my awareness. I was in pure soul form at this point of the ceremony.

I chuckled, "This is ridiculous, isn't it? I had forgotten. Forgotten how divinely protected and guided I truly am."

Of course, I was. The anointing in and of itself was more than enough. How can you see a future that isn't supposed to be yours?

You see, I had been called to leave fitness coaching fully for quite some time. That had been my career for the last decade. I love my athletes; I love my competitors; but the industry itself is something I no longer aligned with.

I had been using "fitness coaching" as my disguise to help people become better leaders and make their own impact on this world. I had just been playing way too small and was too afraid to step both feet into what I knew I was put here to do.

I had been playing small for a universe that only responds to those who play big.

I had recently started working one-on-one with entrepreneurs and aspiring entrepreneurs or even just aspiring humans who wanted to change the world for the better by making themselves better. I was very passionate about this work, as I could physically and energetically feel the breakthroughs in these incredible individuals' lives.

But God told me I was limiting my capacity too much by keeping it to one-on-one sessions. He spoke words and goals into me I had not been able to fathom until coming out of the ceremony.

I took these words and these goals and created the Impakt Legacy Mastermind. At this writing we are in the building phase. It has not been launched yet. But by the time you are reading this, we will be running and open for enrollment should you feel called to join us in helping the collective create a better world.

The numbers and obstacles He wouldn't stop putting into my head were nothing short of horrifyingly intimidating:

1 million people served in this mastermind.

100,000 new businesses born from breakthroughs.

A new facility that can host 5–10,000 people for events and seminars.

Are you kidding me? Are you reading this with just as much disbelief as I had when I kept seeing it as well? These numbers seem supernatural . . . and maybe they are.

All I know is that everything was confirmed for me in the ceremony. I was assured through the endless ocean of love at source that I was doing exactly what I was meant to be doing. I had been praying for the "team" to find me. Calling it into the universe. "Let me tell you what," it answered.

Our team for this mastermind is truly unreal, nothing short of a blessing with God's hand all over it.

We are now equipped with the firepower to carry out our mission.

Our mission is dedicated to bringing in people who know they are meant for more but can't figure out exactly what that is yet. Whether they are eight-figure earners or five-figure earners, we bring people in, build them up, and empower them to be the leaders they were born to be. Ridding them of their past and aligning them with who they truly are and what they were put on this earth to do. We help alchemize their business around their new self so that they can go and make their own impact on the world, building a legacy to leave behind when they are gone.

The anointing of my life to help this world heal through the empowerment of self and building up the next wave of leaders made me want to throw up. I had so much chaos in my heart. I convinced myself it was just spells of anxiety here and there, but until this ceremony, I didn't realize that my heart was aching because I wasn't allowing it to do the one thing that it came here to do: love.

Once I accepted that love was no longer something to fear

but something to wield as a weapon to fight the wounds of the collective and to use to teach people to lead with their scars, it fully embodied me. As if all darkness in me ceased to exist.

> Love is mine.
> Love is yours.
> Love is ours, collectively.

I think it's time we cut the bullshit and get back to what we were put on this earth to do. All we have to do first is surrender to it. Surrender to our ability to tap into a power greater than we can even comprehend. Surrender to the endless power that flows in your veins. When we do that, it will flow through us freely and touch everybody in our lives.

Erwin McManus, in his book *The Way of the Warrior*, also speaks on the concept of the universe being created for us. He teaches that God has no need for the universe; it is created specifically for us. It can exist without us, but we cannot exist without it. The universe is exactly what it is supposed to be in order for life to prosper. I don't know about you, but I can't think of anything that embodies true love quite like something that was made specifically to give us life.

The universe is our home and is filled with endless possibilities of what we can do and experience. The power to wield it lies within our courage. Our courage lies within our capacity to love. Our capacity to love lies within our ability to surrender.

THE THREE STAGES OF ASCENSION

I DON'T BELIEVE IN MYSELF

My external environment was once the sole determinant of my self-worth. If I didn't have someone pointing me in a direction, telling me what to do, and telling me "Good job," I felt as though I had no action to take.

I was sitting around waiting for the world to serve me, to guide me, or to lead me to the next thing that I wanted in life. I felt incapable. I felt unworthy of success. I felt unworthy of love. I learned from an early age that there was never enough and that the true value of a man was measured solely on what he could produce. As such, I never felt like I was enough either.

I was consumed by scarcity. I felt I needed to lie, cheat, and steal my way through life. Money controlled my entire nervous system. Once, in high school, we were at a friend's house for a "kickback" (a party, but not big enough to be an actual *party*). My girlfriend and I were staying in the parents' room that night. About halfway through the party, I went to change into some comfier clothes. As I was changing, I opened up the end table drawer, and in it I saw a Ziploc bag full of $20 bills. My entire nervous system froze. My heart started to pound; my breath started to quicken in my chest. I closed the bedroom door.

Click

I locked the door so nobody would come in. I pulled out the Ziploc bag and took all the money out. With that money in my hand, I felt unstoppable—a massive adrenaline and dopamine rush as I contemplated how many California burritos I could buy with this. I put half the bills in my underwear and put the other half back in the bag before walking back out to join everyone at the party. I was on edge the rest of the night.

I had gotten so good at lying I started thinking fifteen steps ahead of everyone else. I had a feeling that they might notice the money was gone. And if they did, they would surely have everyone empty their clothes, pockets, shoes, etc. I folded the money up and put it in my sock at the bottom of my foot. Sure enough, they noticed the money was gone and had everyone take off their shoes, empty their pockets, etc. They came to the conclusion it had to have been someone who was there earlier. I was in the clear.

The next morning, I got out of there faster than a bat out of hell. I put gas in my car, bought my girlfriend and me a California burrito, and the rest was history.

This wasn't the first time I had stolen. Hell, it wasn't even the twentieth. I was a certified thief at this point. It didn't take long before I had lost sight of who I was altogether. My constant highs when stealing, accompanied by the constant lows of realizing I was the textbook definition of trailer park trash, left me with a story of who I wasn't. But it was a story I now identified with because I didn't know any different.

When we don't believe in ourselves, it's because we don't know ourselves. When we don't know ourselves, we are victim to the first person who gives us an answer. We seek the outside world to validate us.

Matthew McConaughey speaks about the difference between being a nice guy and a good man. I was a nice guy. I was the nicest guy. I was whoever I needed to be, saying whatever I needed to say to put myself in the best position for gain. When I felt guilty, I would go out of my way to make everyone around me happy so that just in case an allegation came up, they surely wouldn't believe it. All I could care about was myself. That's what scarcity does to us. We become selfish because we are stuck in survival. We are still animals at the end of the day, and when we get put back into our animal instinct of survival, we can't be surprised when we act like animals.

A nice guy is always thinking ten steps ahead. He is always saying the right things, manipulating people around him, collecting data to use to his advantage, and putting his wants and needs above everyone else's. A good man is a kind man. A good man will say what needs to be said even if it gets him some negative feedback. A kind man does the right thing for the greater good of all parties involved, not just the thing that he wants for himself. The world is plagued with nice guys. Learning how to energetically feel the difference between a nice guy and a good man is an invaluable tool to develop inside yourself. Ladies, this doesn't just apply to men. Women can be just as deceiving with their actions.

Luckily for me, I was a nice guy for a large portion of my life, so now I can spot them. From a hundred miles away. Every time.

"I don't believe in myself" stems from constantly waiting for others to make decisions for you. It is not an incapability issue as much as it is a simple lack of courage that is holding us back. When we feel fear, we feel incapable. We become frustrated at ourselves for being afraid and then use fear as the reason we are not moving forward. We pour all our energy into this hallucination that is fear. We forget that courage can only exist in the presence of fear. Without fear, courage cannot be brought to life. There needs to be a fear for us to overcome in order to be courageous. So then, where does courage come from?

Courage comes from the heart. The heart is the center of the energy points in the body. It separates our lower three energy centers from our higher three. Think of this as the separation from our lower selves to our higher selves. The heart is the gateway to overcoming our guilt, fear, shame, judgment, etc. It takes courage to open your heart. It takes courage to consciously make choices that bring us closer to love every day.

Personal development and spirituality are great, but I fear they are being overly leveraged. We are all stuck in "I need to be better" mode, and it has made everyone enter into a war with a deficient version of themselves. We have a massively long checklist of all the things we want to work on: limiting beliefs, traumas, mindset, depression, anxiety, stress—the full list would probably be longer than this book! No wonder everyone is so overwhelmed and we don't believe in ourselves. Have you seen all the shit that's wrong with me???

We are asking a million and one questions every day trying to find out how to get away from all the parts of ourselves we hate. It's enough to drive any sane person mad. Now I don't think personal development and spirituality are to blame for this. I think humans are. We don't believe in ourselves, which means it's easier to believe in how fucked up we are. We want to be able to say, "See! This is why I am the way that I am." But that just isn't true. Sure, you can always get better. But you're always worthy of love. In every stage of your journey. Making "better" the gateway to finally being worthy of love is delusional. No wonder we lack courage and belief. How could we not when all we see are the reasons we suck?

I BELIEVE IN MYSELF

Believing in yourself is the next phase of this journey. I have found that most people I work with usually have one foot in "I believe in myself" and one foot in "I don't believe in myself."

This is an interesting phase, one that can be exhausting and frustrating. When everything is going great, life is happy, business is good, and health is amazing, it is very easy for us to believe in ourselves. This is where the foot placement comes into play. We have to use belief when we don't know something to be true yet. Beliefs can be advantageous and also poison for our souls. It's disheartening to witness sometimes. I mean, there are some people who actually believe pineapple belongs on pizza.

We don't actually believe in ourselves; we have just disguised our belief in the external environment as something that seems more woke. We "believe in ourselves" when everything is going our way, and then we lean back into "I don't believe in myself" when things start to go south. So, we constantly battle between being courageous and being discouraged. Loving ourselves and being frustrated with ourselves. I believed in myself every time I had momentum. Almost to a fault. I felt unstoppable, like a god. I was the man. Then once things would crumble and fall, I'd lose myself in the ruins.

This phase, however, is the most important and also the most painful. I think we have to rise and fall multiple times because in the course of hitting rock bottom and "losing it all" over and over, you start to develop something spectacular: belief. Losing everything starts to become significantly less earth-shattering the twelfth time it happens. Sure, it sucks, and it isn't exactly a picnic, but you build fortitude in this phase. You build self-awareness, you build groundedness, you build discernment, you build character, you build the real you again.

You know what happens next? You start to trust yourself to handle the tides of life, and in that space of developing trust, you develop love for yourself. You need to be very careful when you start knocking on the door of this immense power inside of you; once you do, your life will never be the same again. This is why most people keep themselves from walking through the door. To walk through the door into radical self-love and trust means that everything in your life that has been anything other than love has to be given up.

Alchemy is something that has always been fascinating to me. The Law of Equivalent Exchange states that humankind cannot gain anything without first giving something in return. To obtain anything, something of equal value must be lost. Okay, maybe that was just a condensed quote from *Fullmetal Alchemist*, but the principle is the same. Something of equal value must first be lost.

I find that wording so incredible.

This law is guiding us into the path of experiencing loss before we experience gain. Most of us immediately say, "Fuck that." We don't want to give up what we currently have before we see the next lily pad we can swim to. This often leads us to ride a sinking lily pad until we are fully underwater and drowning. Our life turns into a constant lack of oxygen. Nothing we have breathes life into us anymore as we slowly suffocate into a state of depressive dissociation. We are so afraid to experience loss that we slowly lose our lives in the process.

Once I understood this law, it didn't make the pain of loss easier. What it did for me, however, was crack open my ability to trust something greater than myself. It forced my hand to surrender. To look someone you love in the eyes and tell them you need to let them go, knowing that it means you will be fully alone, is terrifying. Knowing that they will go be with another. Imagine the instant ego spiral: What if they find someone better? What if everyone says they've "upgraded"? What if they forget all about me? What if they move on immediately, and it proves to me that I meant nothing? I can't see them with someone else. It will kill me.

So, what do we do? We hold on. And when we hold onto things that are no longer meant for us, we are behaving no differently than a toddler throwing a temper tantrum. The universe is always moving and shifting things around to put us exactly where we are supposed to be. If we fight that force and continue to hold onto something or someone that no longer serves us, the only thing we are keeping in place is ourselves. The universe will continue to move things around; if you do not allow yourself to be moved with it, you will continuously find yourself in situations that turn out to be in your worst interest. You will experience more loss, financial hardship, plateaus, frustration, betrayals, all of it, over and over.

The universe is gentle but powerful. It will try to inflict the smallest amount of pain possible first to try and help you let go so it can move you to somewhere you belong. The more you endure, however, the more the pain starts to increase. The bigger the catastrophes, the higher the stress, the deeper the pain.

You'll start to lose trust in the universe or God because you have created the story that the world is out to hurt you. You believe yourself to be worthy of what is happening to you, so you continue to anticipate the next bad thing. Anticipation is an act of creation. You are co-creating the experience whenever you anticipate it. You can't stop thinking about it, you act in ways that are aligned with it already happening, and eventually *poof* there it is.

"I can never catch a break," we say, unknowingly reinforcing the story that it will now, surely, happen again. It cracks me up because I still do the same thing to myself. Man, we are so powerful, and we direct all our thoughts in ways that act against ourselves. It's impossible to believe in yourself when you are stuck in this illusion of powerlessness.

The Law of Equivalent Exchange is a law that governs a large part of my life now. The interpretations I have for it are this:

> Your old life for your new life.
> The old you for the new you.
> Your old relationship for the new relationship.
> Your old business for your new business.
> Your old stories for a new story.

Which means we have to be willing to stand in the face of loss, emptiness, and uncertainty for an *undetermined* amount of time before we receive the exchange. Yikes. Belief can only get us so far under this law because what this law really requires is *trust*.

Contrary to the collective perception, belief is not an act of trust—it is merely an act of hope. It's nothing more than wishful thinking. When you believed in Santa Claus as a child (spoiler), you wouldn't sleep the night before Christmas. You battle nerves wondering if he would come or not. Where there is *only* belief and hope, there is a level of unrest. There is a level of anxiousness, a level of ungroundedness, and a lack of assuredness. So, you can see how relying on whether or not you believe in yourself as the catalyst for taking action is hindering your ability to create the life you desire. We cannot both believe in something and know it to be true at the same time. Belief is nothing more than the final stepping stone into knowing.

I KNOW MYSELF

The final ascension in this three-part process. It is the space that finally emerges when we have overcome the need for belief. Let's go back to Santa Claus for a second. Now, you know what really happens on Christmas. You know that you buy presents for your family and that they buy presents for you. You know that you'll all gather around the tree, enjoy the time together, and have breakfast. There is no anxious anticipation for whether or not you will experience the full joy of Christmas when you go to bed the night before. You sleep well, and you rest assured that when you wake up, you will be at your destination.

The act of knowing creates a ripple effect of peace throughout every cell in our bodies. We know that trauma is distress without resolve. So, what would resolve be in this illustration? It would be a full-spectrum understanding of what happened and why. When we look back at our pasts, our triggers, our traumas, and our stories, the reason they still control parts of us in the present is that we still don't understand the full perspective. If we did, we would be able to put it to rest and move on. We believe we know what happened to us and why; therefore, our justification for why we are the way that we are is nothing more than wishful thinking.

When you finally discover who you really are and know yourself, it is impossible to not look back on everything that has happened to you—mistakes you have made, people you have hurt—and feel anything but gratitude and understanding. The day it all clicks and you just . . . "know" what it all meant. That's the day your life really begins because it's the day you finally experience wholeness. Everything else is simply another journey before that journey. You stop rushing and feeling as if you're falling behind or wasting your life. What a silly thought, to sit in the middle of a life you are living and convince yourself that you are wasting it simply because you are on part of the journey you are uncomfortable or dissatisfied with. The fact that you are not satisfied with being on the journey, wherever that currently is for you, is the exact reason why you are stuck. You have lost trust in the divine timing of life and the nurturing guidance of the universe. When you know that what you want has already been created and is waiting for you, the journey becomes a lot more exciting.

Let's say you are five years old. Your parents told you that you were going to Disneyland during summer break. But Disneyland never came, and now you're back in school. You're upset, you're cranky, you're unsatisfied with the car ride every morning, and each day that passes you feel even worse about where you are. Friday morning your mom tells you that you need to wake up an hour earlier than normal because she has to drop you off early before a work meeting.

You wake up pissed off. You get in the car pissed off. Your mom starts to drive, and all you can think about is how awful the future is going to be when you get to school early. Your whole mood is off. You're stressed and angry at the world.

Then Mom turns around and says, "Guess what? We're not going to school . . . we're going to Disneyland!!!" and in a split moment your entire worldview, energy, and attitude instantly shift. Now the car ride is filled with satisfaction. Now you wish you would have woken up earlier so you could be closer to the destination already. You're sitting in sheer excitement now, fully satisfied in knowing that you are getting close to what it is you want.

Mom may have to pull over to get gas, but that's no bother to you because you trust where you're headed. You trust that your mother will get you there exactly when you're meant to. Maybe she also pulls off to grab some food, but that's no bother to you because you're in no rush! You're just happy to be on the journey. Your attitude dictates your direction.

Now let's look at this from the way most people go about life. Mom says, "We're going to Disneyland." Most people say, "Oh, why today of all days? I'm busy today, can't we do it next week, do you know what traffic is going to be like?" and this list goes on and on. Now you're in the backseat, and you start to get impatient with your mother.

"Seriously, we still have another two hours before we get there?? Can't you drive faster? I should already be there!"

She needs to pull off to get gas . . . "Seriously Mom, why wouldn't you have filled up the tank yesterday before we left? Now we are driving the exact opposite way of where I want to be going. This is such a waste of time!!" Your mother gently explains that if you don't travel off the path at times to get the proper fuel, you will never make it to where you want to go.

Sometimes the path straight forward isn't the direct path to where you want to go. There are times we need to move sideways to go get gas, or eat, or learn a lesson, or gain a tool of wisdom, or maybe a change in perspective before we can get back on the road and make it further. Sometimes we need to change a tire, fix the engine, or stretch our legs. If your mother was anything like my mother, if I bought a piss-poor, ungrateful attitude toward a trip to Disneyland like that, as I was yelling about being impatient and how she needed to provide me what I wanted faster and better . . . she would have 1) probably smacked the shit out of me, but more importantly 2) she would have turned the car around to go back home.

I can hear her now in my head: "When you fix your attitude, then I will take you to where you want to go."

If you haven't caught on yet, the current version of you is the child, and the mother is the universe. The universe is nothing but energy and vibrations. Your attitude governs both of these elements. The better your attitude, the more grateful and satisfied with the journey you are, and the faster your mom drives you to everything you desire. The worse your attitude, the more ungrateful, impatient, and unsatisfied you are with life, and the faster your mom turns around to take you back to your starting point so you can relearn the lesson.

When you learn to know that everything you desire has already been made for you, and that's the only way you were able to actually think about, envision, and desire it in the first place, you start to relax a little bit.

"But it can't be that simple. That's just a woo-woo scam," thinks the reader who still relies on belief alone to change their life.

I don't believe in what I am saying or writing; I know it to be true. You can know something else to be true that completely opposes everything you just read—that's our incredible power as creators. I know that what I want and my attitude toward the journey directly correlate with how much I have of what I want.

When you know yourself, you begin to trust yourself. When you begin to trust yourself, you fall in love with yourself. In that space of love for yourself is the devotion to enriching that life and making life better. How could you not? When you fall in love with someone, all you want to do is enrich that love. You buy them flowers just because it's Tuesday, you show them off on social media, and you praise them to all your friends.

So how can we give all of that to ourselves? By changing

our heart and expanding its capacity to love. When you fall in love with somebody, you fall in love with their heart. You fall in love with who they are when you finally know them, and nobody can take that away from you. No matter what someone tells you about their past, who they've been, what they've done, you will tell them, "You don't see what I see in them."

When you can finally say that about yourself, nobody can take that away from you. You know your heart, and you have fallen in love with who you are.

Every day we must make a conscious effort to know ourselves a little bit more. In order to know ourselves, we have to tap into our highest actualization of self. Which is love. Anything that is not love is not you. Making conscious efforts every day to bring ourselves closer to love is bringing us back home to ourselves. This might look like stepping into an elevator with someone else and, instead of staring into your phone, asking them how their day is going. Maybe you compliment the jacket they're wearing or offer my favorite compliment: "You have great energy."

This can look like taking the time to ask the cashier at the grocery store about their day and making them laugh. It can look like setting boundaries for yourself, taking yourself out on a date, buying a meal for a homeless person, or going out of your way to make someone smile. The list of ways to bring us back to love is endless.

ASCENSION TASK

I want to offer you an invitation. That invitation is for you to take the next seven days and go all in on consciously choosing actions, thoughts, and decisions that only bring you closer to love. By the end of those seven days, I can promise you that you will feel addicted to making people feel loved because of how loved it makes you feel.

Write down a list of ten acts of love you will devote yourself to every day for the next seven days. Maybe you will tip your barista $10 every morning, buy your wife flowers, compliment a stranger, have an intentional and fully present conversation with someone you care about, etc.

This reminds me of one of my favorite quotes ever from Dr. Joe Dispenza: "The love you give is the love you receive. The pain that you feel is not from love being withheld from you but from the love you are withholding from the world." That means we are the ones solely responsible for how much love or pain we feel in our lives.

"This guy is fucking insane," your ego bellows.

Yet the inner you, the highest version of you, knows it to be true. That's why you felt a sensation in your body when you read it. That's the truth. The truth is sensational. We feel it.

The closer we get to love, the closer we get back to who we actually are. The more you do that, the more you remember who you are. You no longer have to rely on believing in yourself, believing in God or the universe, or even believing in love. You know it to be true because it is who you are. When that happens, you become the divine and abundant being that we all have inside of us. All you have to do is remember your story, your identity, your patterns, and your choices.

CHAPTER 7

ABUNDANCE

You have to *choose* a life full of blessings and abundance. It is not something that gets bestowed upon you from a higher power, because you are the conduit for all of these cosmic and godly forces in your life. You have to open yourself up to it, or the energy cannot flow.

Abundance is a portal that flows *through* you, not *to* you. For abundance to happen in your life, things must flow both to you and from you. By holding onto anything good or bad, you shut yourself off from the channels of abundance and call it bad luck.

SCARCITY IS AN IDENTITY

When I was growing up, money plagued me. I had to do a lot of things to stretch my dollars and "keep up" with my friends in high school. I drove a 1999 Pontiac Sunfire. At the time, $20 filled up my entire gas tank. I was always finding ways to make more money. Scarcity looks different on everyone, but the underlying sense of panic for survival is a human law when we are in this state. It is impossible not to think selfishly when you are in scarcity. It says nothing about you as a person if you are in this state and all you think about is yourself. I've been there, and I understand.

When animals in the wild are attacked by predators, they all scatter and flee. They do not stop to make sure the other animals in the herd are safe, because the standard default is fight or flight. Our evolutionary default is not to protect and think about others before ourselves when danger is presented. That is something that has to be reprogrammed over time.

In high school I learned how to hustle in a lot of ways. Whenever there was a house party, I would ask the person throwing it if I could clean up the entire party in the morning before everyone woke up in exchange for keeping the cans and bottles. This gave me a place to sleep for the night, and it gave me enough to take to the recycling plant in town to make $10. At the time, it would usually be enough for me to get a California burrito for breakfast and put the remainder in my gas tank so I could drive home. My mom usually gave me $20 for the week for gas to get to and from school, but that obviously was never going to cover all the Four Lokos we were drinking every weekend.

When I moved out, I had to improvise. I would lie, cheat, and steal my way into the perception of what I thought safety was for me at that point in time. I became an undercover con man and a thief. I would bum my friends' couches and beds until I had overstayed my welcome. Once I ran out of couch rotations, I would just sleep in my car in the Kmart parking lot after my shift until I could go to the gym and shower the next morning before heading to college.

If I was driving into town, I knew the exact hill I needed to get to going seventy miles per hour. If I hit it right and there were no cars in front of me, I could put my car into neutral and coast through the last eleven miles of road all the way into town, saving even more gas for the weekend shenanigans.

I wasn't an unhappy kid, but I wasn't exactly a happy one

either. My weekends were spent blacking out, drinking the hangover away, and getting into random fights at the beach I couldn't even remember afterward. I would punish myself with alcohol. The sicker I felt, the more I drank. That was the identity I had fallen into.

That was the version of me that was accepted. That was the version of me that got invited to things and felt included. I needed to be the "party animal" in order to get my needs of connection met. My party trick was usually grabbing a handle of vodka and chugging it in front of the entire party. Embarrassing myself was my go-to because if I could just give up my dignity, I would at least have friends. This was a truth that I came to believe about myself and my life.

When you are operating from a place of needing to perform in order to maintain friendships, you constantly need to seek more friends. Eventually you lose who you are entirely and have to rotate friend groups after they've known you long enough and you run out of material for your character to play. Maybe it becomes a massive fight or some other "reason" for the friendship to end so you can get back to safety. On to the next show for you to perform. That was me. The performer. The actor. I had worn a mask for so much of my life I didn't even look at my face when I stood in front of a mirror because I had no idea who I would see.

I was making mistakes, but the scarcity I was living in was a driving force behind my actions. Abundance can be just as dangerous. That's why it is the last step. You have to be ready for it, or it will destroy you.

THE ONE THING YOU CAN'T HAVE

The three pillars of the human experience we all know to be health, wealth, and relationships. When we see someone with all three of these in balance, we can't help but idolize them. From my experience, I see that most people can juggle two of them well, but the third seems to be their biggest frustration. Maybe you're in an amazing relationship and top shape, but you can't seem to find that financial breakthrough no matter what you try. Maybe you're wealthy and in perfect health but just can't seem to get love right.

If you nodded your head to the latter, then I am just like you. Success has always come "easy" to me. Okay, maybe not easy. Business was just an easy thing to "click" in my brain early on in my career. The more work I put in, the more I get out. Just like the gym. My physique was my first real obsession as I came up in the bodybuilding community. I've built up some serious confidence and proven track records in these areas. I can usually get in the best shape of my life within six weeks; I can start a new business and have it profitable in a few months, every time.

When it comes to love, however, I always seem to fall short. I still have yet to figure it out. Every time I experienced a new love, it would feel like I was getting closer and closer to the actualization . . . and then it would fall through. One relationship, I'm not present enough, so in the next I try to overcompensate . . . and then I'm overly present, which comes off as needy. We all hear the same shit cooked up over and over by the "gurus" and motivational speakers who tell us, "Love yourself first. Then you'll find that partner." Is that really true, though?

I can happily say that I love myself, but I still don't feel complete. Maybe I'm wrong for making love my biggest motivator in life. I think we all have that feeling with our lowest "pillar" . . . the one we struggle with the most is the one we want the most. Love has always been the number one priority in my life. I've always wanted my own family.

So why can't I seem to figure it out? At this point my heart has been broken so many times I'm surprised it still holds a beat, but I fight for it every single day. Love is about opening yourself up to another and being fully seen. Letting somebody else have all the power in the world to destroy you and greeting them, arms wide open, with trust and surrender.

So why does love scare me so much? I can't be the only one who feels this way. Why do my wide-open arms always end up emptier than before I opened them? It feels as though every time I let someone in, they take more of me with them when they leave. But when you've been the common denominator enough times, it eventually feels impossible not to entertain the thought that maybe you're unlovable. Maybe there's some karmic contract my soul is meant to play out in this life . . . where love is never supposed to come to stay. To test my devotion so that I can have it in every life following this one. This is my lifetime of loss. Those are real thoughts I used to battle inside my head.

Is life worth living if you don't have the one thing you would die for? Why do we create a wall of separation from the one thing we want more than anything else? Why do we convince ourselves every day that we aren't good enough to hold it? That we aren't worthy of it?

What's the point in withholding yourself from the endless possibilities in this life out of fear? What are we so afraid of? Pain?

I used to be afraid of pain. I would avoid it at all costs. Until I realized that the pain was how I knew that the love was worth it.

Even for the short time I was able to hold onto it. I've come to love the pain because I know it is a necessary part of my life. Without it, I cannot appreciate what's in front of me. And that's the shitty part, isn't it? You never really understand or take in what is right in front of you until pain has shown you what no longer is. Pain is a greater force than love. With love you can become blind, but in pain you see everything. Every inch and corner of the truth. You see exactly who you are, exactly what you love, and exactly what you fear. Pain is the best teacher—not because of the wisdom but because of its ability to show you exactly what is important to you . . . even if it's no longer yours. At this point I'm not really sure why I'm writing this section in the book. Maybe nobody feels the same way I do. Or maybe one of you reading this feels the same way, and now you don't feel as alone anymore.

The truth is that a man without love is not a wealthy man. A man without love is as poor as they come. A man will buy and buy and buy and hope that something he buys will be life everlasting. The only thing that is life everlasting is love. Not money, not fame, not legacy . . . love. Ask me any day of the week: I would trade every penny to my name for love. That's what frustrates me the most.

It's like the one thing I would commit my life to I can't commit to once it's in front of me. I put up walls, I create stories in my head, I retreat, I create distance, and I hopelessly watch as the love slowly fades away with each kiss. It is the slowest and most painful of all deaths a man can experience. The death of a love that you thought would be yours forever. It doesn't matter how much someone loves themself; when you lose someone, a part of you dies with them.

I'm honestly tired of self-help books pumping into everyone

that you should never care if someone leaves you or stays because you have to focus on yourself. Of course, you have to focus on yourself and build your own dream and have your own goals, but guess what? When you reach the top of the world and turn around to find no one standing next to you to share it with, what's the point? What is the point of life if not to share it with another? What good is wealth without a partner to spoil? What good is optimal health and living a longer life if you have nobody to share a longer life with? What are you building right now if not something to share with another?

You can't sit here and convince me that this life is meant to be focused on yourself. Maybe I'm a helpless romantic. Maybe I'm too obsessed with love, but then again, what's worth being obsessed with if not love? If I offered you $10 million today with no strings attached except that you could not spend a penny on someone else and you would never wake up next to someone you love for the rest of your life, would you take it? What if I offered you $10 million right now and the only catch was that you wouldn't wake up tomorrow?

If you answered no to those, then you just showed that having someone in your life and even the simple act of waking up in the morning is more valuable than all the money in the world. Yet we convince ourselves we are miserable because we lack money. We are missing the point of what it means to be alive. We are missing out on true abundance.

HOT COFFEE, ICED COFFEE

Imagine a hot coffee and an iced coffee an hour after you bought them. Both have gone from their "extreme" original temperature and resolved into the ambient temperature of the room. Most people (myself included) would now throw their coffee away; other people save theirs for home, where they can either warm it up or add more ice. We call these people sociopaths.

What this observation unlocked for me was just how many people experience the same things in their lives. When life is an extreme experience, we can't get enough. We wake up early, make more phone calls, move more, smile more, connect more . . . the list goes on. For this example, we will dictate hot as "good" and cold as "bad" for illustrative purposes.

When life is hot, we continue to push forward like nothing can stop us. We are on a hot streak, and everything just seems to "click" . . . for a few weeks maybe. Then we start to slow down. The voice in our head starts to return, telling us we have done good, but the other shoe is about to drop. Then creeps in the self-doubt, the excuses, and all the reasons why we can't keep the momentum . . . so our life begins to cool off. Our life comes back to "room temperature," and we are no longer invested in experiencing all it has to offer.

We pull back, and it eventually cools down to ice cold. Now we are at the other end of the extreme spectrum—scarcity, mental health in the gutter, ruled by anxiety, getting a second and third job "just for a little while to be responsible," gaining body fat, new medications to help "manage" the symptoms we don't seem to "have an answer for," and we get sucked right back into the rat race. That life is designed to keep us on the wrong end of the extreme experience spectrum so we are easier to control, less likely to rise up, unable to become the hero of our own story, a lifelong recurring customer for "help" as we become reconditioned to wait for someone or something to come rescue us.

Allowing your life to cool off is the worst thing you can do for yourself. Everybody wants balance until you realize that balance brings you right down into the unfulfilled extreme. Everyone wants "just enough to be comfortable" until you realize you are selling yourself short of your God-given potential, which is a massive disservice to Him, yourself, and everybody you are meant to be helping in your life.

I am a hard believer in living life hard. Making sure I stay piping hot for as long as I possibly can. I am notorious for drinking my coffee alarmingly fast. Once it cools, I no longer wish to experience it. I live my life the same way. When I originally started writing this book, I was just going to document some hard shit I've been through and how I got through it in the hopes of helping someone else who is feeling as helpless as I was.

What I didn't realize was how many other people and stories I have encountered in my life so far that proved to me why you can surrender but you can never give up. You can surrender to your circumstance, but you cannot allow your life to cool off. You can never allow yourself to sit and accept your current situation, because there is always a way to heat it up and get the fire back in your heart. I hope some of the stories I share in this section will help you relight the fire of abundance in your heart and help you realize who you are and just how much you have allowed your life to cool off. With all the love in my heart, I know you can do this. I know anybody can do this . . . because I have proof.

214 FITNESS

Names and titles will be slightly changed in this story so I don't get sued, since that's the world we live in. Anyway . . .

When I was in college, I was working multiple jobs trying to make ends meet. Four jobs, a full-time college workload, after-school participation, and a 1.5-hour commute both ways from school to home while maintaining a six-day-a-week gym routine. I wanted to break out of the system so badly that I found myself fully enslaved to it—thinking I needed to get my college degree to have authority and credibility in order to get work. Convincing myself I needed to sacrifice all the time in my life to making money instead of easing up to enjoy life once in a while. I was mostly focused on a dance major at the time, although I was also studying kinesiology and oral communications. Dance was all I had known ever since my mom enrolled me in my first jazz class in sixth grade. I hated it. Somewhere in the abyss you will find a VHS tape of me "leaping" across stage in a sparkly blue tank top and matching pants. I found myself very drawn to the hip-hop scene as I walked past a few of the hip-hop classes at the studio. From there I turned it into a passion, hobby, and income stream by teaching hip-hop classes and choreographing wherever I could.

As I made my way to college, I started developing a very strong passion for fitness. I started personal training people at the high school football track in Ramona. It wasn't the most consistent or professional setting when it required my clients to climb over a seven-foot chain-link fence from time to time. It wasn't sustainable, but it was getting me clients and experience and expanding my word of mouth. I started copy-and-pasting (when you could still do this) the same message about offering workout plans and meal plans for $100 on Instagram profiles—spamming before I even knew what that meant. I was hungry, and I knew I was good at what I was doing.

I got my ISSA (International Sports Sciences Association) certification program completed in about two weeks. It was surprisingly easy to blow through, but I had already been obsessed with learning as much as I could on my own. This is a place I see a lot of entrepreneurs fall short: waiting for a certification before they start becoming experts in their skill or field. You should be expanding your expertise, even if there isn't a piece of paper waiting for you on the other side.

Eventually word got around my little town of Ramona that I was getting results, and good ones. I spent months juggling my heavy load and answering "frequently requested questions" on my Instagram. Not a single soul asked me a question for four months . . . I made the questions up myself because I knew the information would be great. At the time I did not understand the concept of just putting out information for whoever needed it, so I felt the need to pretend that the question had been asked . . . but hey, it worked as it needed to.

I came into contact with another personal trainer through a friend in our town who owned a small training studio. When we met, he explained to me that he had found a much larger building and was transitioning into opening a full-time gym. My eyes widened as he spoke of needing a partner in the process to get it up and running. When he offered me to partner with him and to help me build my personal training roster, help run a gym, and come on full-time, I couldn't believe it. Nineteen years old, and I'm going to be a co-owner of a fucking gym? Where do I sign?

Nowhere. I was nineteen and took everyone's word as assured backing in business endeavors. Ignorance is bliss until it isn't.

Over the next few months, I started taking on more clients. I dropped out of college to give it my full attention; now I had no other option but to make this thing successful. He would delegate tasks to me to get the gym ready while he trained his full roster of clients. I understood why I needed to do a large majority of the work . . . he was busy and funding it, so it made sense to me.

We finally made the full transition and opened up 214 Fitness to the public. I was overwhelmed with pride and accomplishment. I couldn't help but walk around tall with a smile on my face at everyone who walked through those doors.

After a few weeks, the membership numbers were steady, the gym was profitable, and my personal training roster was full. I was making $30 an hour in sessions and loving every second of my life. I would work the gym unpaid from about 7 a.m. until closing at 10 p.m. Monday through Friday and whenever needed on weekends. I was happy to work these hours unpaid because I was a "co-owner" according to a verbal agreement between two men. Until one day I was pulled into the office and sat down . . . I would become very familiar with the look of darkness in his eyes over the next few years.

"Is there a reason you feel you can walk around telling everybody you own my gym?" he asked me aggressively as he leaned toward my face with his.

I frantically started explaining to him that I never meant for it to seem that way and that I made sure to always say "co-owner" or reference "our gym." He cut me off.

"*Our gym*? This is my gym. When did you become co-owner? You are the manager of this gym, and that is your role. You are not an owner."

Puzzled, confused, and slightly shattered, I timidly agreed and apologized. Then he let me out of the office. As the night went on, I started to think more about this "manager" title (that I still didn't think to ask for a contract around) and figured I should ask him what the compensation structure looked like for that. To my surprise again, I was bullied into submission and was made to feel awful for thinking that I expected to be paid when I was being allowed to keep 100 percent of the money I got from my clients.

I had no real idea how this worked at the time, so I assumed I was in the wrong. I guess that did seem pretty fair. When I did the math, essentially being at the gym an average of seventy hours a week and thirty of those being personal training sessions (that I had to stop whenever someone was at the front desk), I was making about $12.85 an hour as a full-time manager and personal trainer.

"Okay, I guess that's not too bad . . . I love the gym, I love my clients, so I guess this is just what my life looks like now." A few other trainers came on during this time, and we all got along super well. We all shared the same fear and anxiety placed around our boss and the cage he called an office. That office was a very confined space, like being trapped in a cage with an animal you don't want to be in a cage with. I witnessed many sexual affairs with his clients inside that office. Eventually we just knew to stay clear when the door was locked and the blinds were closed.

A few months went by. Since I was the one running the gym as "manager" and was there the most, I developed a lot of rapport and respect with our members. They all started referring people to "Nick's gym" because they assumed I was the one running it (I was). When wind of this got back to the boss man, it was back into his office. Door closed, blinds drawn . . .

Okay, I know what this means . . . He's either going to bitch me out or try to make love to me.

He got into his stance and grilled me for calling it my gym again and started to list off all the complaints we were getting from members of the gym about me. Which I knew instantly was a bunch of BS, since I was the only one at the gym for them to complain to in the first place. Needless to say, this was the reasoning for stripping me of my manager title and demoting me down to just head trainer. At this point I was fed up with his shit, so I was pumped.

"Okay, so that means once I'm done training my clients for the day, I can go home, right?"

"No. You still need to work the same hours, do everything you were still doing, and manage the other employees' work schedules for the weekends."

Oh.

It is a very interesting position to be in as a man when you have been constantly belittled, emasculated, and disempowered. You start to just take the punches in the hopes of avoiding as much conflict as possible. So, I bowed down again and agreed.

One weekend my girlfriend and I were almost down to the beach, which was about a forty-five-minute drive for us, when I felt my phone ring and saw his name. We all know that feeling . . . when you see their name and your stomach falls into your ass and your heart jumps out of your throat.

"Oh fuck," I said.

When I answered, I was informed quite loudly that one of the employees didn't show up for their shift, and he needed to go home. So, with my tail between my legs, I pulled off the freeway and turned around to go back and work the next six-hour shift. This man controlled every aspect of my life, and I was allowing it. I was helplessly relying on him to stay afloat, so I felt I had no choice but to be his little bitch.

Eventually, enough was enough. I started looking around at gym equipment online and spoke to the other trainers about my pull to leave and open my own spot. They all jumped at the idea of getting out from underneath the shoe of our boss, so with us all in agreement, I began looking for potential investors to help us out. I was determined to get everyone over to a better place as soon as possible.

I learned very quickly to mind whom you speak to around situations like this. One of the potential "investors" I spoke to was one of the lovely housewives our boss was having an affair with (it was hard to keep up). It didn't take long for her to inform him of what I was asking her about.

At 9:47 p.m. on a Sunday night, with clients I was supposed to train the next morning at 5 a.m., the trainers and I received a group text letting us know to cancel all further appointments at 214 Fitness and to come get our belongings.

I felt sick, like my legs were going to crumble into dust beneath me. I drove straight to the gym with my girlfriend at the time to confront him. When I pulled up, I watched as a thirty-year-old man scurried into the back room of the gym to avoid me and left his mom and dad to handle the affairs instead. I grabbed my stuff and went back to my place. If it wasn't for my girlfriend at the time being as supportive as she was, I really don't know how I would have made it out of there. I was freaking out. I started calling friends, friends' parents, anybody I could think of that had some sort of gym equipment at their house or in their garage. Something was better than nothing, and I did not have the time to be picky. That next morning, I began sending texts to all my clients, who had already been informed of my removal by my now-former boss. I will say, as helpless and directionless as I felt at that time, it was ten times better than dreading walking in the door of that gym every day.

ON TO THE NEXT

I remember training my first client of the day, Tracy. Tracy was a spunky woman and a hell of a firecracker. We always made each other laugh. As I was training her outside a friend's house in their backyard, it started to rain. My eyes followed suit. I had no idea what I was going to do. All I knew was that the only path to travel was forward. I vowed to myself that I would never find myself working for another man again. If I went homeless, it was on me; if I made it, it was on me. From here on out. No matter what.

One of the other trainers ended up finding a friend of a friend who had a separate garage in their backyard with "plenty of fitness equipment," and he agreed to allow us to train our clientele out of it until we figured out what to do next. I was so proud to hear that every single one of my clients said they were following me wherever I went. That was the first time I really caught a glimpse of the power you can have when you serve your people to the highest of your capacity. Loyalty like that has always been something I strive for, and damn did it feel good to have a little bit of traction and security under my feet again.

As I walked into this "garage gym," I saw one wrestling mat (cut in half), a squat rack with a rusted barbell and two twenty-five-pound plates, a few uneven DB sets, and one kettlebell. I couldn't help but laugh. It wasn't much, but it was a hell of a lot better than where we came from.

We ended up training our clients out of this back garage for over a month as I kept searching for an investor and a space to rent for us. It was winter, and the nights inside that uninsulated garage were piercing. Yet I managed to grow my personal training clientele in that environment. I was in a place twenty times smaller than my old place, with less than a fraction of the equipment, and I was still gaining clients. I really had proved to myself that my circumstances had nothing to do with my success or failure. I just simply had no other choice. Subway is always hiring, but the thought of going backward into a "stable" job didn't even exist in my mind. All I looked for were ways to make my business succeed, which I believe is the only reason that it did. Eventually we got a call from the third trainer who worked with us at the gym saying he had an investor. It was his father-in-law, and he had agreed to write us a check for $20,000 and asked if that was enough to build a fully functional gym.

"Yep, that's more than enough," I said.

Absolutely the fuck not, I thought.

But it was something, and something was better than nothing. As the time came closer to pick up the check, I had already met with a landlord and signed a contract for a 1,600-square-foot warehouse space. It was an old furniture store with incredibly low ceilings, broken up into multiple rooms. Again, something was better than nothing. Then the conditions of the investment came into play (at the last minute), and the father-in-law only agreed to give the check to us (me) if I agreed to make his son-in-law a 50 percent partner in the business. I immediately felt blindsided by what felt like a betrayal. Now I see the practicality behind making sure your daughter's husband is making a good chunk of a business if you are the one saving it with your money. However, the thought of me allowing another person to make decisions over me again after what I had just gone through was never going to happen. I nudged hard, and we finally agreed on a 55/45 split, so I still had the majority say. I had no choice but to sign and get into the building. I had no time to spare.

I searched every fitness equipment website for hours on end, multiple shopping cart totals in the notes on my phone, making new shopping carts on six different sites every night to find every possible penny I could pinch while still creating a presentable gym for the public. I ordered everything with no warranty to save money, ordered every piece for "curb drop-off," and denied any professional installation whenever I could. As pieces came in, the other trainers and I spent hours putting together the gym while my partner remained nowhere to be found.

Was I about to let yet another man ride the wave of my efforts without putting equal in? Absolutely not. So, I made the decision (our space made it for me, really) that we would not be opening for members. The only cash flow to be made would be what we made personal training, and that income was "outside" of the actual business income. There was a lot of tension around the "partnership" regarding the gym. I knew very little about business and how a company needs to be run in order to be successful. We were all severely lacking in leadership, humility, and directionality. Over time we worked up to five trainers renting out space and all pitching in on rent. I ran a supplement store out front to make a little extra money, and things were good! Sure, it leaked and flooded when it rained, didn't have any heat or AC . . . but it was (partly) mine. In the summer I would soak through about three shirts a day from sweat and drink about 2.5 gallons of water. Ramona got very hot in the summertime, and the intensity of winter was no different. We ran NK Fitness for a little over three years before moving on from it.

THE ONLY PATH IS FORWARD

I continued posting my fitness content on Instagram and had developed some friends around the San Diego area that I met up with for workouts and to film content from time to time. My YouTube channel was my main priority for a while; I was fully immersed in the fitness space at this point. In 2017, I attended the Arnold Expo in Columbus, Ohio, and stayed in an Airbnb with a bunch of other fitness personalities.

After a few gym sessions and conversations at our house, I was asked if I would be willing to coach three of them for bodybuilding shows. Never saying no to any opportunity, I said yes. I had never fully thought about what an online coaching position would look like or even how to offer that service. I offered it to them for free to get some exposure and experience under my belt. It did not take long before the results started speaking for themselves. I started getting inquiries for online coaching flooding into my DMs.

I started coaching people for $150 a month from my cell phone. It was all done via text, and I had separate "albums" for each of my clients so I could reference their prior week's photos. I had no idea what a "system" even was for business, but I started signing clients left and right.

Today I help entrepreneurs with their development and the creation of their business. I hear a lot of excuses in my line of work. I always hear how people "can't take action" because they don't have the perfect website or don't have the right name, they don't know how to create systems yet, etc. Look, I started an online business with only my cell phone and a skill, just like 90 percent of modern entrepreneurs. Convincing yourself you need everything set in stone perfectly to start a business is a perfect excuse to keep you from taking action—and keep you living a mediocre life.

I started having some scheduling collisions. I was at my gym at 5 a.m. every morning, and I was the last one out at 9 p.m. every night. My online check-ins were starting to eat up my entire Sunday, as sending back and forth text messages for client check-ins is very time-consuming. I started to realize how much larger my reach was supposed to be. I started hearing a voice wake up inside me, telling me that I needed to get out of this small town.

When I thought about my future thirty, forty, or even fifty years down the road, I pictured myself still running my gym there. That scared me. I knew I was in the wrong place. It was time for me to make a move, or I never would. You have to reach a point of no return, a point where looking back is more terrifying than looking forward. I was at that point. Within one month I had made my decision, sold off the equipment from the gym with just enough to pay back the remainder to our initial investor, and I moved to an apartment down in San Diego, right next to Qualcomm Stadium. In less than one week, my income had dropped about 50 percent without personal training . . . and my living expenses had basically doubled.

Most people in a situation like this usually look only through one lens. It typically comes down to a few key questions most seem to ask themselves:

Where can I cut back?

What expenses do I need to lower?

How can I save more money to create security for myself?

In my opinion, thinking this way brings you the opposite of security. Operating from scarcity can only ever bring you more scarcity. This was a paradigm shift that completely catapulted my life and wealth all around. When we operate scarcely, it does not matter what happens to us financially. We get fifteen new clients, and we assume it was luck, so it will never last . . . we need to be smart and save the money. You get handed a check for $50,000.

If you've been operating out of scarcity, what will you do with it? Either keep it all in your savings account or blow it all on "investments" that you need to make now that you have money.

You see, I believe that overspending and underspending are the same problem. I believe they both stem from scarcity and a lack of trust in our capacity to handle or deserve wealth. No matter how much money we make, our lives never change because we live in the fear of losing it all. Whenever you focus on how much you need to save or the things you need to reduce because you just can't afford them right now . . . you have a mirror showing you what your life will continue to look like over and over again.

The only question I asked myself at this point in my life was, "How can I produce more?"

All I gave my energy to was seeking how to improve my situation instead of cowering and hoping for the storm of scarcity to pass. My energy and focus needed to be channeled into the right direction in order for me to truly break into a brand-new way of living for myself.

It still strikes me as odd that most people see investment in themselves as an expense. All that tells me is that they do not have the trust within themselves to make a return on any investment they make. They blame a coach or a program or a business or a circumstance. Anything they can do to get the spotlight off of them and bring back the victimhood that enables them to never push forward and change their lives. I thank God every day that this is no longer me and never will be again.

I went all in. I either succeed, or I become homeless. Sure, I could have gone back and lived with my mother, but that still wasn't even a possible outcome in my mind.

Over the next year, my online coaching presence exploded. I

coached more competitors than I ever thought. One of the first clients I took on from that Airbnb went on to win her Pro Card (which in the bodybuilding world means you can now compete at the professional level; it's a big deal) in our first competition season together. I was obsessed with growing my team and winning. When I was approaching the one-year mark and our apartment lease was coming up, I started to look at my options to see what my next move was now that I had created a stable income for myself.

I nearly passed out when I finally took a second to analyze my finances and realized I had the ability to . . . buy a house?

I have never needed much from a living space. Growing up in a small trailer and a little wooden add-on attached to it, I was raised in more of an enclosed style of living. The "shitty" apartment my roommate and I lived in at the time was the nicest place I had ever lived. I was in disbelief of having a two-bedroom apartment and my own door to my room. I could have lived there forever and been ecstatic. I really had no idea what it would even feel like to live in an actual house. I called my good friend James Visser (a real estate agent from Ramona), and we began the search. I knew nothing about the process of buying a house, and everyone warned me how much of a nightmare it was. To my luck, James helped me find a home I loved, and within thirty days of me saying "this is the one," the deal was closed and he handed me the keys.

A year prior, I had walked away from my gym, which was making me a profit of about $2,500 a month. Now I was putting a $60,000 down payment on a home. It felt surreal to me. Going through that experience with a friend like James made it even more memorable and special.

I will never forget the day I went to that home for the first time as "mine." James was already there waiting for me. I parked my car, and he handed me the keys and said, "She's all yours, buddy!" He got in his car to head out. As I stood at the front door (my front door) for the first time in my life, my hands were trembling so much I could barely get the keys in to unlock it. I walked into my empty house and sat down on the kitchen floor and cried with gratitude and disbelief. The first house I've ever lived in, and I'd bought it myself. I say "myself" loosely, because there was just no way any of the things I've accomplished in my life would have been possible without every person who has trusted and supported me. If you are one of those people and are reading this book right now, I just want to take a second to say thank you. You have no idea what you mean to me, and I am forever grateful for every one of you that has crossed my path.

As the next few years rolled on, the team grew. I was able to hire coach after coach after coach due to our team's increasing demand. Less than two years after buying my first house, the company was doing seven figures a year. Abundance.

Today I have shifted away from the fitness coaching business and dissolved it to allow myself the free range to serve others as I see fit within my evolution of self. My time in the fitness space will hold such an incredible flame in my heart. I don't know if I will ever truly be all the way out, as I still have a handful of competitors that I love coaching with all of my heart.

Looking back at where I started with 214 Fitness, being locked in a cage to be yelled at by a boss who showed me the exact opposite of leadership could have been the best thing to ever happen to me. I think a lot of times people freeze from action due to not knowing exactly who it is they want to be. Having the ability to experience someone who is the exact opposite can be a blessing because it allows you to at least know which direction to start walking. I can't imagine what my life would currently look like had I rolled over and given up just because my circumstances seemed impossible to overcome.

What I never realized was that it is actually *me* who is impossible to overcome. The world does not promise that nothing will stand against you or try to knock you back or turn you around. What I promise you is that when you give yourself no option but to keep moving forward, you start to knock things down that are standing in front of you. It is incredibly easy for us to ease off when the fire gets too hot. We wait for things to cool back to room temperature. For some of us, that is the path we will drag ourselves down our entire lives, wondering why we continue to break, wondering why we don't seem strong enough to push forward and make that change.

You are a victim because you have forgotten that room temperature is not what forges steel. If you want to claim what is meant for you in this life, you are going to have to surrender to the suck of your situation. Surrender to the fact that it's hard, that it's not going to be fun, that people and circumstances are not always going to be there to help you. Surrender to all of that so you can push through regardless. If you do not walk into the fire, if you give up the second you start to feel some heat, then you will continue to live your life scarce and at room temperature, disinterested in experiencing it because there is no excitement.

All it takes is for you to accept surrender—and never accept defeat. If I can do it, the little boy from a trailer park in the mountains, raised by a single parent, surrounded by kids my age turning into drug addicts, with no exposure to breaking out of a system and creating a life of one's own . . . you can do it too. Otherwise, what's the point?

UNPACK YOUR BAGS

By the time I finish this book, I will be wrapping up my twenties. In my twenty-nine years, I have never felt like I was "home," no matter where I was. I always felt like I needed to be on watch for the next ship to jump to, the next plane to catch, the next "thing" to run toward.

It's June of 2023 right now, and I am spending the majority of this month living out of my suitcase. Jumping from state to state and country to country is a blessing and also extremely frustrating. Not feeling grounded because I don't have my home base, normal routine, or "home." Yet, that's how I've always lived in some capacity. Out of a suitcase. Never committing to my life enough to unpack my bags and do the work to make my life feel like a home.

I would always convince myself that where I currently am is not enough, and I need to be rushing toward the next phase of life. Maybe this is where I find my salvation. Maybe when I finally get "there," I can unpack my bags and settle in. I've never allowed myself to take off all my armor and breathe, never once sat on my bed and not thought about my next move, and never once celebrated anything I've ever accomplished in my life, because I'm too focused on moving "on to the next one." Now don't get me wrong, this mentality has gotten me extremely far, and my life is nothing short of a blessing. While all that is true, I can't help but observe the emptiness that comes from lacking depth and intimate commitment. Is this abundance?

We love to keep a suitcase packed just in case. We don't want to put both feet in. We want one foot in and one foot out. This way we can lean in when it's good and lean out when it's bad. No matter which way we lean, it always ends the same . . . feeling torn and unfulfilled. We want to commit only when it's a sure thing. I don't want to fully commit to the relationship because what if they leave? I don't want to go all in on my business because what if it fails? I don't want to go all in on my life because what if I . . . ? What? Struggle? Die?

What I have learned the hard way (and by that, I mean over and over and over . . . and over again) is that 99 percent commitment doesn't create success. You have to be 100 percent in if you want the story to become true. I find it fascinating that we have a hard time believing that could be true, yet we are 100 percent committed to the story of our suffering and live it every single day. It is not our story that is powerful; it is our *belief* in the story that is powerful. When you believe your life needs an escape plan, you will live it out of a suitcase.

What other areas in your life are you not committing to? Keeping one foot in and one foot out, just in case? What would happen to those areas if you decided to unpack your bags and make them feel like home? Building a home requires work.

When you live life out of a suitcase, you have nowhere to live and no chance to feel alive. This leads to a lot of shallow relationships.

What area of your life doesn't feel like home currently? Take away the position of something outside of you being at fault and internalize the feeling. Why are you tolerating your lack of commitment to the life you say you want? What are you unwilling to sacrifice to get it? You either sacrifice for what you want, or what you want becomes the sacrifice. You go all in, there is sacrifice involved; you don't go all in, there is sacrifice involved. There is sacrifice no matter which way we choose to look . . . what's on the other side of our sacrifice is our own choice.

So how do we finally stop living out of a suitcase and unpack our bags? Well, we stop running. From life. From ourselves. From love. We surrender to the abundance that has yet to find us. We stop putting on a mask and pretending to be somebody we are not. We take off our armor and show up vulnerably and bravely. We look life in the face and open our arms wide, fully naked, and close our eyes as we lean into a deeper trust than we have ever known. We open our palms to the sky, and in doing so, let go of everything we've been holding onto. Open palms are the gateway to receiving, and we spend our entire life with our palms closed, holding onto the past for dear life. You want to make your life feel like a home? Let go, lean in, commit to it fully, and surrender yourself to the power greater than all of us. Love.

STANDARDS FOR OUR LIFE

We have high standards for life. We want more money, we want better service, we want faster delivery from Amazon . . . the list goes on. Our standards for exceptional experience continue to go up, while our standards for exceptional effort continue to go down. Our world is a spinning paradox. We expect others to behave in a way that we ourselves don't. We expect perfection from those we follow. Social media personalities, celebrities, and people of "higher" perceived status have been stripped of their humanity because the world has been stripped of its common sense. We are turning humans into gods and perpetuating the cycle of our own unworthiness by comparing ourselves to a false image we've created for people we know absolutely nothing about. We escape from the incredibly harsh self-judgment we levy on ourselves when we find someone else we can judge just as harshly for making the same mistakes.

"Oh, but they're in the public eye! They should know better! Shame on them for being human!"

Maybe we should all know better because we are all still human. I'm all for winners and losers, first-place trophies, and no participation trophies, but we also cannot lose sight of the fact that we are all imperfect humans chasing a perfect image. It's destroying humanity, and now we are celebrating dysfunction instead of embracing higher standards. We are rewarding mediocrity at an alarming rate because it's more comfortable for us to be mediocre.

We keep success at arm's length because we don't want to commit to the effort necessary to achieve it. Which means we never achieve anything, and the things we do achieve become unfulfilling. Why is that?

Well, what's more impressive to witness, the training or winning the trophy? Most people are more inspired by the trophy. You don't see the NBA Finals being replaced by live clips of the teams practicing. That's because spectators, the ones in the seats paying for a ticket, do not understand the work and sacrifice that goes into being great. The NBA knows nobody would watch all the hard work the players put in; we only watch them on game day and let them know how awful they are if they miss a shot. But great things only happen in the aftermath of great sacrifice.

What do you think is more rewarding to the one who wins the trophy? Is it just winning the trophy? Or is it winning the trophy after knowing they put in the hardest work they've ever done? The harder the effort, the sweeter the victory. We've lost touch with reality when it comes to what it means to have victory. Now we think victory is getting an influencer canceled because they accidentally misspoke while talking live on a social media platform. We walk away with our heads held high, knowing we ruined someone's entire life because they were human. We sacrifice time and spend more effort creating anonymous profiles online to bash people in the arena than we do on creating a life we actually enjoy. Our standards are high for everyone except ourselves, and that is why we are so unfulfilled. If great things aren't happening in your life, if abundance is dodging you, I can guarantee you that you aren't sacrificing the right things.

ONE QUESTION TO RULE THEM ALL

Love and fear are not exactly "polar opposites." Fear is merely the absence of love. Love is trust—deep understanding and trust at our core level. If you're afraid of the dark, you're not actually afraid of the "dark"; you just don't trust what might be lurking. Maybe you are afraid of relationships and love, but you're not actually afraid of them; you just don't trust them because you've been hurt.

You see, love cannot exist without trust. Which would mean that if we don't love ourselves and believe in ourselves, it would boil down to the simple fact that we've stopped trusting ourselves. And if how we feel on the inside dictates what we get on the outside, it is no surprise that we continue to attract people we can't trust and who don't love us back, or circumstances that leave us feeling like helpless victims, which reinforces our lack of trust for ourselves.

"Is this going to bring me closer to love or further from love?" That is the golden question and the secret of abundance. A question that has become my North Star. Making conscious efforts everywhere to act closer to love has changed my life in indescribable ways. As Joe Dispenza said, "The pain that most of us feel is not because of the love that is being withheld from us; it is from the love we are withholding from others." We don't trust ourselves anymore because we have forgotten who we are and *what* we are.

If God—you know, GOD—if God is unconditional love, then that would mean he created everything *with* love. Only love.

If God created everything with unconditional love (yes, even you), then . . . where did everything else come from? Where did anger, hate, depression, anxiety come from?

The ego. From humanity. From us losing our way and cutting ourselves off from the love (trust) of God and the universe. If you have cut yourself off from the love that created everything, would you be surprised that your life currently sucks? Would it really be that shocking to live a life of constant stress and unfortunate events? A life that feels as if love is lacking? Well, that's because it is. It's lacking because you forgot who you are, and the second you remember is the second your energy comes back to you.

Remember your assignment from Chapter 6? Take the next seven days and make conscious and disciplined efforts to ask yourself the question, "Will this bring me closer to or further from love?" Ask it in everything you do. Put your phone down to be fully present with your friends, partner, or family. Actually listen to them. Tip your barista an extra $5 because her vibrant energy "made your day."

I started making this a conscious habit for myself, and you know what happened? It became almost impossible for me to not feel love in my life, love for myself, love for other people. I am like the Energizer Bunny on crack now with how abundant my energy has become. I have felt my heart get bigger and my capacity to love expand wider than I ever knew possible. But it's not just energy. Since I started applying this habit, I have had more opportunities, connections, offers, business, and friendships come into my life than I can even believe. I am filled up with love and generosity because I practice getting myself close to love every single day.

The craziest part? Nobody is doing that but me!

The closer I get back to love, the closer I get back to myself. Which means the more I lean into knowing love, believing in love again, the more I can begin to know myself again too.

ABUNDANCE TASK #1

Take in a big breath through your nose. Now breathe in a little bit more. Fill up your belly, then your chest. Now hold at the top. Feel how your head starts to feel like it may explode, maybe your heart starts to beat harshly as you feel your nervous system get a bit panicked. It might be hard to even read these words now, but we will exhale in just a second.

Three . . . two . . . one . . . exhale.

Now take a big breath in and then return to your normal deep-breathing cadence. Slowly in, all the way in through your nose, and slowly out, all the way out through your mouth. Continue this and feel peace and well-being return.

Next, take a huge breath in again through your nose. Now, audibly exhale it all through your mouth. Keep pushing all the air out. More. A little more. Stop there and hold at the bottom.

Notice the sensations in your nervous system as you hold or close off your lungs. Hold it just a second longer.

Three . . . two . . . one . . . breathe back in through your nose and return to your normal deep-breathing cadence. Slowly in, all the way in through your nose, and slowly out, all the way out through your mouth.

At any point, did you fear letting go of the air you were holding onto at the top? At any point, did you fear that when you finally took a breath in, the air wouldn't return to your lungs?

Probably not. But did you notice that you only felt peace when your breath consistently flowed in *and* out?

When we hold at the top or the bottom, we cut off the flow of oxygen, the flow of abundance. If you receive (breathe in) money and hold onto it all, it starts to cause problems. If you give (breathe out) money and hold onto the fact that it's gone, it starts to cause problems.

Life, business, finances . . . it's all a game of breath. When we can unlearn attachment and relearn flow in any part of our lives, we start to find ourselves in a continuous state of peace, gratitude, and well-being. There is no need for attachment or possession in someone who is abundant. Just like there is no need to push the person next to you away for fear that they are breathing up all the air.

Any breathwork enthusiast will support practicing your breathing to increase your lung capacity over time. A list of the positive effects of increasing your lung capacity would be almost as long as this book. The one that always stands out to me is that increased lung capacity extends your physical stamina and results in greater health overall. Healthier lungs (increased capacity) lead to a more robust supply of oxygen, which fuels healthier cells. If we tie the concept of abundance and breathing together like we did during this exercise, we can see the similarities clear as day. To increase your lung capacity for a better life with healthier cells, you must practice every day by taking full breaths that push your boundaries a bit, and then you must let all of that air go, then repeat multiple times. Do it every day.

To increase your capacity for abundance, you must practice

the act of abundance. Allowing yourself to receive or "breathe in" wealth: money, praise, love, opportunity, material goodies, joy, friendship . . . all of it. Every time you feel your capacity filled to the brim, you breathe it all out and give everything back into the universe. Let all of it go, just like you do with your breath. Once you've given it away, you begin the process all over again, filling yourself up with new wealth, opportunity, love, and friendship—and once again letting it all go. This is how we increase our capacity for a life of abundance.

ABUNDANCE TASK #2

It is very easy to make a long list of the things you don't have. We often place all our attention and energy on where we are lacking in our lives and thereby create even more separation. Most people don't realize they are creating more of the things they are trying so desperately to "escape" by doing this. It can be almost impossible to shift out of a low-vibrational attack when you're the one doing the attacking. Let's fix that.

For this exercise, you will need a pen and a few sheets of paper, preferably in a notebook. We are going to do a few different variations of this exercise to really help shift your energy toward a new reality altogether. Ideally, you will add a new step to this exercise every morning over the next few days.

> **Step/Day 1:** Write a diary entry recalling your day as if you are writing it before bed. Focus on all the negatives that you constantly think about. For example, "Today I woke up and noticed that I didn't have $10,000 in my bank account. Then I went to the gym and picked myself apart for about an hour, noticing how out of

shape and undesirable I am. After that I went to Instagram and scrolled in envy as I gossiped in my head about other people who have what I want. I chose not to take ownership of my projections and instead decided that anybody more successful than me must have done something immoral to get there. Once I had a few moments to sit in my anger, I decided to go for a walk and think about how soon rent was due and how stressed or anxious I am."

Get as specific as possible. You might find it slightly uncomfortable to put some truths on paper—truths about how you've been going about your life unconsciously—but that's exactly why we're doing it. Once you have finished this diary entry, read it once aloud to yourself and then simply go about your day. Take note of what starts to come up for you as the day progresses. What are you starting to notice in yourself? What thoughts are no longer slipping past your consciousness now that you've written them down? Are you becoming more aware of the stories you reinforce in your own head throughout the day? Make note of this on the adjacent page before you go to bed.

Step/Day 2: Write a diary entry the same as the first (in the morning, but as though you are recounting your day before bed), but this time focus on everything that you wanted to happen. For example, "I really wanted to meet someone special today. I would have loved it if I'd bumped into a stranger, and it had turned into a love story. It would have been a pleasant surprise to run into a lump sum of money that randomly came my

> way. I wish I would have gone to the gym and thought about how much progress I've been making and given myself some praise for how hard I've been working."

Once you have finished your new diary entry in specific detail, read it out loud and go about your day. Make note of what new things start to come into your awareness. Are you noticing things differently than during yesterday's exercise? What specifically? Any change in your energy or awareness? Make note of these throughout your day, and then write them down on the adjacent page before you go to bed.

> **Step/Day 3:** Write another diary entry the same as the others, but this time recall your day as if everything that you wanted to happen did. For example, "I met someone really special today. I bumped into a stranger, and it feels like it might turn into a love story. It was such a pleasant surprise running into a random lump sum of money! I went to the gym and noticed all of my hard work starting to pay off. In fact, I actually think this was the best I've ever felt in my body."

Once you have finished this journal entry, read it out loud just like the others, but really allow yourself to feel into that day emotionally. Feel the gratitude and joy from each of these events as you reflect on them already having happened. Once you are done, tuck your journal away and go about your day. When you make note of your day this time . . . how different does your energy feel? Do you notice you are more open to conversation with people? Are you more present and on your phone less? Are you actively more aware of confirmation for the day you've already experienced? How much differently do you feel on this day compared to the first day? And the second? Write your reflections down on the adjacent page again.

> **Step/Day 4:** Start over from Day 1 and go through the progression of this exercise again. Continue to make notes at the end of each night if anything else changes. Once you have completed the second round of this exercise, landing you on Day 6, choose which diary entry or reality feels the best to you. Once you decide, make a promise to diligently rewrite and speak out loud that same day every morning for the next thirty days. Energetically and emotionally feel into the events as if they are happening as you are writing. At the end of these thirty days, you may very well find yourself with a completely different energy and a completely different reality.

ABUNDANCE TASK #3

Abundance is a byproduct of generosity. We must be generous before the universe is generous to us.

Take a desired monthly income goal that you have for yourself. In this example we will use $50,000. Write this income goal at the top of a sheet of paper titled "Desired monthly income goal."

From here, shave a 0 off the end of that number until you reach a number that you are able to "give" at this moment. Starting at $50,000, ask, "Do I have the capacity to give this amount away right now?" If the answer is no, drop off a 0. $5,000. Ask the same question and repeat until you find a number that gives you a yes. Say you land on $50. That is the amount you are able to give away this month in your current situation.

Turn the piece of paper over and write "Desired monthly contribution goal" at the top instead. On the first line of the paper, write the current month. August: $50. Write out the rest of the following months. Now set your desired monthly contribution goal equal to your desired monthly income goal. What we are doing is shifting your focus away from how much you want to get and placing it on how much you want to give. After the $50 goal is hit, the next contribution goal would be $500 in a month. As you continue to climb up the ladder, you will get to $5,000 and then eventually $50,000. Can you imagine what your monthly income will be when you are able to give away $50,000?

The most important part of this exercise is to make sure that you are giving your contribution in a way that feels good to you energetically. You must give it in a way that brings you joy and gratitude for being able to do so. Maybe you buy clothes for a family in need. Maybe you donate to a charity you feel connected to. One of my favorite things to do is to get $200 in $20 bills every week and hand them out to workers, baristas, or even strangers just to see them light up. When I was younger, I was living off an $800/month paycheck. Now I make sure to give that amount away every month in cash as a reminder of how far I've truly come in my life.

There is nothing more abundant than being able to generously give to those around you. It makes me feel incredible to do so. The more we give, the more we get—a fundamental law of the universe we would all do well realigning ourselves with. Soon enough you will shift your energy and focus from monitoring your progress by how much you make to monitoring your progress by how much you are able to give. When you can do that, numbers start to matter less and less while people start to matter more and more.

When people are finally more important to you than money, you will have everything you need and then some.

CONCLUSION

I've been in the process of writing this book for almost two years now. It's no coincidence that these have been the two most transformative years of my life. I have battled with deleting this book and starting over close to fifty times. Each new version of me considered the words of an older version unworthy of bringing into the world.

As I read through the pages now, I see and feel the growth I've had as a man while writing it. I see the words that were being called to me through God at every stage of my healing journey. Whenever I got the urge to write, I would. Seeing the accumulation of these breakthroughs is quite the experience.

The truth is, when I started writing this book, I was not fully surrendered. I wanted to write a book as a means to claim the status of being a published author. I was writing the book for myself, to build a monument to show the world, "Look at me, look at what I've done."

I can't help but laugh at my ignorance. I love the duality of someone wanting to egotistically write a book titled *Surrender* in the hopes that people would pick it up and not see right through the massive layer of bullshit inside it.

I'm so grateful for all the "writer's block" that seemed to

invade my mind whenever I tried to write from that space. It was as if I became incapable of writing when I was rigid and uptight—or scarce in thinking I needed to write this book as a symbol of my own acknowledgment for the life I have lived. As if my experience of it all wasn't enough.

I would go months without the drive or motivation to write anything at all, and then I would get hit with waves of thirty-, forty-, or fifty-page vomits out of nowhere. It felt like each time I made my way back to the book, I had already been given a brand-new life while still having the memory of my old one.

That's where I think personal development and spirituality are starting to severely hinder people. Yes, they are built with good intentions and have changed millions of lives, but everything has a dark side. We are now equipped with the ability to find everything "wrong" with us or the parts that we should improve. We can all draft a bullet-point list of our shortcomings in under a minute, but we can only stare at a blank piece of paper when it comes to making a list of what makes us amazing. This is where we are losing sight of our humanity. Global adoption of "1 percent better every day" has put us in a constant war with a version of ourselves that we've deemed deficient. It's uncommon to love yourself because we only understand what being at war looks like. Humans understand war more than we understand peace.

Every time I was at war with myself, I couldn't write. Nothing could flow through me. Every time I was at peace with myself, I couldn't write fast enough. I was open and soft. I was relaxed for receiving. It seemed like everything flowed through me effortlessly.

Still, I would sit to write again, and I would see all the deficient parts of my older self and wonder what deficient parts still lingered in the present. I would think that maybe I should put off writing this book until I had experienced more life or was "more healed," more credible, more qualified. I struggled to see the older versions of me as worthy—but God always did. At every stage He gave me downloads to write; at my darkest hours He still spoke with me to remind me how worthy I always was.

The writing of this book uncovered many shadows in the way I treated myself and the way I was treating other people. It was so easy for me to take an older version of people at face value and damn them for eternity, never giving a second thought toward someone's true worthiness or ability to evolve. I wanted to define people by their past; it's obvious why I was still defining myself by mine. God never did that to me. Even in all the years when I was out of alignment, as far away from Him as humanly possible, He waited.

We think we are without love because we have shut ourselves off from love. Love is around us at all times. Gently waiting for our call so it can flood in and hold us. Love is not forceful; it does not rush, it does not manipulate, and it does not judge. It simply waits.

I've laid out the steps, methods, and stories in this book that have helped me and hundreds of my clients reach a state of surrender. I've seen people overcome insurmountable odds, experience indescribable breakthroughs that changed their lives in an instant, and receive unexplainable overflows of abundance in their lives once they finally surrendered. Nothing can be changed in your life until you decide for it to change.

The day you make the choice to change your perspective on life, on your power, and on who you actually are is the day you start to experience the rest of your life as a miracle. It's the day your life actually begins. Surrender is freedom, it is power, it is abundance. Surrender is the gateway back home to the source.

My hope for this book is that it finds the people who are meant to read it, which would be *you*. Let this be the sign that shows you that you are ready for your next life to start. The sign that it's time to let go of your old stories, let go of the people who no longer serve where you are heading, and let go of all your belief in your limitations. This is your time to surrender all of those to God and let the universe move you to where you need to be.

Unclench your jaw, relax your eyebrows, take a deep breath into your belly, and hold it at the top. I want you to feel the release of everything that no longer serves you when you let out the exhale from your mouth. Hold it just a little bit longer, and when you're ready to release, do so with love and do so with intention. Set the tone for how the rest of your life will now be lived out.

You will no longer *need* to worry, but you sometimes will. You will no longer *need* to judge people, but you sometimes will. You will no longer *need* to be angry, but you sometimes will. At the end of the day, no matter how much you surrender, you will still be human, which means you will mess up, you will make mistakes, you will hurt people. None of that makes you a bad person. It just means you're human.

I want to extend a show of appreciation to you for picking up this book and reading it to the end. I battled my ego during the publishing process as I considered sharing such intimate stories from my life. I hope it was as positive for you reading it as it was for me writing it. Thank you. From the bottom of my heart. Sharing my journey with those who resonate brings me more joy and purpose than I could ever put into words.

I hope that this book showed you that we are all a lot more

similar than we are different. I hope that you can own your truth now in a way that empowers you to shape your life accordingly. I hope you offer yourself forgiveness and compassion. I hope you acknowledge yourself fully for everything you've overcome, and you remember how powerful you are. I hope we can connect after you're done reading this book if something resonates with you. Please shoot me a message on one of my social platforms! (I use Instagram the most.) If the book impacted you positively, I ask you to take a few moments to leave a review to help others find it as well.

I had to learn a new way to surrender my life over and over again because I didn't understand what it meant to surrender. The path to your final surrender can only be walked by moving through the tumultuous anointing process of life's struggles. Without struggle you cannot build character, and without building character you cannot be trusted with a better life. You are going to make mistakes, you are going to hurt people, you are going to feel ashamed, you are going to feel defeated, and it is going to feel helpless at times. These struggles happen to everybody; the only difference is whether we choose to be consumed by them or choose to overcome them. Every time you overcome the next hardship, you build faith and an inner sense of who you are becoming. You bring yourself closer to God every time you triumph over a struggle that was sent your way. You will eventually realize that you only ever needed to surrender once.

You need only surrender your life once when you surrender it to God. Your vibration rises, your energy increases, and you begin to operate at a new frequency. The day you surrender your life to God is the day you become eternal. When you surrender, the only possible outcome is the one that's best. You just need to give it enough time.

ACKNOWLEDGMENTS

Thank you to God for putting me in places that I didn't understand at the time and to forge me into the man He intended for me to be. Thanks for every lesson learned through pain and every breakthrough experienced through love, for continuing to bless me with a voice and a stage to carry out the mission entrusted to me for this lifetime.

Thank you to my mother for giving me everything she possibly could have during my childhood.

Thanks to the little trailer-park kid who never backed down when life challenged him, and for taking every punch on the chin and moving forward regardless.

To all of the friends and family I have been so fortunate to experience, even in the smallest of encounters. Each one of you played an important role in my evolution. Thank you. I would not have the life I have or be a version of me that I now love without every single one of you.

ABOUT THE AUTHOR

Nick Komodina is committed to mentoring entrepreneurs, helping them bridge the gap between spirituality and business so they can create a life they love.

An entrepreneur himself for thirteen years, Komodina opened a gym at the age of twenty-one after spending the first nineteen years of his life living in a trailer park with his mother in the mountains of California. He ran the gym three years and decided to close the doors and pursue a career in online fitness coaching. Within another three years, he grew that business into a multi-seven-figure company that included clothing and supplement brands.

Komodina has been a guest speaker on many stages and has mentored many masterminds. He serves the leadership community in many ways, including hosting RISE, a three-day in-person event where he helps entrepreneurs come back to the present moment and remove any blocks that are holding them back so they can recalibrate to their purpose.

Never one to sit still, Komodina is now producing music, a passion he has discovered in wanting to help people of the world process more of their pain through song.

@NICKKOMODINA @NICKKOMODINA_OFFICIAL